T0316689

Cambridge Elements ≡

Elements in Politics and Society in Southeast Asia
edited by
Edward Aspinall
Australian National University
Meredith L. Weiss
University at Albany, SUNY

POPULISM IN SOUTHEAST ASIA

Paul D. Kenny
Australian National University, Canberra

CAMBRIDGE
UNIVERSITY PRESS

University Printing House, Cambridge CB2 8BS, United Kingdom

One Liberty Plaza, 20th Floor, New York, NY 10006, USA

477 Williamstown Road, Port Melbourne, VIC 3207, Australia

314–321, 3rd Floor, Plot 3, Splendor Forum, Jasola District Centre, New Delhi – 110025, India

79 Anson Road, #06–04/06, Singapore 079906

Cambridge University Press is part of the University of Cambridge.

It furthers the University's mission by disseminating knowledge in the pursuit of education, learning, and research at the highest international levels of excellence.

www.cambridge.org
Information on this title: www.cambridge.org/9781108459105
DOI: 10.1017/9781108563772

First published 2019

A catalogue record for this publication is available from the British Library.

ISBN 978-1-108-45910-5 Paperback
ISSN 2515-2998 (online)
ISSN 2515-298X (print)

Populism in Southeast Asia

Elements in Politics and Society in Southeast Asia

DOI: 10.1017/9781108563772
First published online: November 2018

Paul D. Kenny
Australian National University, Canberra

Abstract: Conceiving of populism as the charismatic mobilization of a mass movement in pursuit of political power, this Element theorizes that populists thrive where ties between voters and either bureaucratic or clientelistic parties do not exist or have decayed. This is because populists' ability to mobilize electoral support directly is made much more likely by voters not being deeply embedded in existing party networks. This model is used to explain the prevalence of populism across the major states in post-authoritarian Southeast Asia: the Philippines, Indonesia, and Thailand. It extracts lessons from these Southeast Asian cases for the study of populism.

Keywords: populism, political parties, democracy, clientelism

ISBN: 9781108459105 (PB), 9781108563772 (OC)
ISSNs: 2515-2998 (online), 2515-298X (print)

Contents

1 Introduction

Populist leaders are currently in power in several of the world's most populous states and are on the brink of it in many others. Southeast Asia has been no exception to this general trend: the Philippines, Thailand, Indonesia, and arguably Timor-Leste and even Myanmar have all seen populists come to power in recent years. Yet in spite of the pervasiveness of populism in contemporary Southeast Asia's democracies, the region remains neglected in the comparative study of populism. Not only are there relatively few comparisons of Southeast Asian cases of populism against those in other regions (but see Hadiz 2016, Kenny 2017, Moffitt 2015, Phongpaichit and Baker 2008, Swamy 2013), but there are also few comparative analyses of Southeast Asian cases amongst one another (for exceptions see Case 2017, Hellmann 2017, Pepinsky 2017, Thompson 2016b). This is both an unfortunate gap in our knowledge of Southeast Asian politics and a missed opportunity to advance our understanding of the nature of populism and the reasons why it thrives in some places and times but not others.

My goals in this Element are explicitly comparative: I draw on the insights of populism studies elsewhere in the world to set out a conceptualization of populism that travels to Southeast Asia; I develop a theory that can account for the prevalence of populism across the major states in post-authoritarian Southeast Asia: the Philippines, Indonesia, and Thailand; and I extract lessons from these Southeast Asian cases for the broader study of populism.

The meaning of populism continues to be much disputed (e.g., Moffitt 2016). A central aspect of the debate is whether populism should be understood primarily as a political ideology or as a type of political strategy. There is of course no *true* definition of populism any more than there is a true definition of democracy or justice. What we need therefore is a definition of populism that is useful. A useful conceptualization of populism should adequately distinguish between positive and negative cases *and* facilitate the development of theoretical and empirical research. The first part of this Element develops what I call the *organizational* approach (see Section 2). This approach has its origins in the writings of German sociologist, Max Weber (1978), and has historically been the predominant way of understanding populism outside Western Europe (Di Tella 1965, Germani 1978, Mouzelis 1985, van Niekerk 1974, Weyland 2001). I define populism in this sense as *the charismatic mobilization of a mass movement in pursuit of political power.*

The idea that populism is a form of charismatic leadership of the masses implies that populist movements have two chief characteristics that set them apart from bureaucratic or clientelistic parties. First, authority within a populist movement or organization is arbitrary and concentrated in the person of the leader. The leader is not constrained by organizational rules and has (near) total authority over personnel and strategic decisions within the organization. Populist leaders can and do utilize *followers* such as party cadres, members, and volunteers to mobilize support; but such followers are characterized by their loyalty to the leader rather than to a party. Thus, populism is distinct from regular party politics on the one hand (where rules over the distribution of authority are important), and mere independent or personalist politics on the other (where leaders lack such arbitrary control over a mass movement or party).

Second, and relatedly, populism is about the mobilization of the *masses* toward political ends. The people, or rather a large mass of them, are critical to any understanding of populism. Unlike conceptualizations of populism as an ideology, however, the concern in this sense is with how the people are politically incorporated, not with what they or their leaders believe (Mouzelis 1985). The people who become supporters of populist movements are mobilized less by clientelistic ties or membership in aligned party or civil society organizations than they are by a direct affinity for the leader. Although mobilization by loyal party activists is not precluded by definition, the direct mobilization of supporters by the leader through mass rallies and the mass media is critical to populist mobilization in a way that distinguishes populist parties from either bureaucratic or clientelistic ones (Kenny 2017).

In contrast to populist political organizations, bureaucratic parties are characterized by rules and procedures governing the distribution of authority within the organization and a range of institutionalized relationships with supporters externally (Panebianco 1988, Sartori 1976). Civil society organizations like unions, churches, and nationalist associations form the bedrock of such parties. Clientelistic parties engage in a quid pro quo with supporters in which support is exchanged for particularistic material benefits (Chandra 2004, Eisenstadt 1973, Eisenstadt and Roniger 1980, Hicken 2011, Scott 1969, Stokes, Dunning et al. 2013). Such parties are governed internally according to factional strength, itself determined by which groups can mobilize the most resources and blocs of clients (voters) (Landé 1965, Schmidt, Scott et al. 1977). Populist movements or parties thus organize the pursuit of power differently to bureaucratic and clientelistic parties (Mouzelis 1985).

The main contribution of this Element is to build a theory of why populists in this organizational sense are successful in Southeast Asia. For reasons explored further in Section 3, while it draws on survey evidence, it concentrates on explaining the structural factors that make populist support more likely at the aggregate rather than individual level. Existing macro-level theories, either developed out of particular Southeast Asian case studies or from the broader Latin American and European experiences, point to a variety of causes of populist success including economic distress, whether due to long-term shifts in the economy (Autor, Dorn et al. 2016, Roberts 2014b) or short-term crises (Weyland 2006), and demographic shocks, especially due to immigration (Evans and Chzhen 2013, Kaufmann 2017, Mudde 1999, Rydgren 2008). None of these explanations works particularly well as a general model of populist success that travels across time and space in Southeast Asia.

The main theoretical claim of this Element is that populist mobilization thrives where ties between voters and either bureaucratic or clientelistic parties do not exist or have decayed. This is because populists' ability to mobilize electoral support directly is made much more *likely* by voters not being deeply embedded in existing party networks. Populists attempt to establish direct relations with voters. This means that they employ frequent public appearances, mass rallies, the traditional mass media, and, increasingly, social media in connecting with voters. Although all political parties make use of such instruments to a degree, populists rely *primarily* on these direct connections rather than party members, sympathizers, or paid brokers to deliver votes for them. This lowers the *costs* of voter mobilization faced by populist organizations relative to other types of political party. Unlike the leaders of patronage parties, populists don't need a nationwide system of brokers to mobilize votes.[1] Analogously, unlike bureaucratic parties, populists don't need the deeply institutionalized links with supporters through interest groups and other civil society organizations that take many years to build. Populism is thus an efficient (low cost) form of political mobilization where bureaucratic and centralized clientelistic party building are inhibited.

Southeast Asia thus provides fertile territory for populist mobilization. Across the region, as indicated by survey data from the Asian Barometer, there is a general a lack of trust in and identification with political parties (Figure 1) (see also Tan 2012). In Indonesia, the Philippines, and Thailand, only three to four respondents out of ten trust political parties. In Indonesia in 2011, seven out of ten survey respondents identified with no party, while that number had risen to over eight out of ten in 2014 (Muhtadi 2018); in the Philippines in 2017, the figure was nine out of ten. It is in such contexts, where parties do not have enduring corporate identities with persistent and

---

[1] As I explain further in Section 3, independent presidential candidates can build a loose network of brokers and their clients. In such a case, however, a candidate is dependent for her support on the loyalty of these brokers. A populist on the other hand, does not rely on such brokers, giving her much greater freedom of action. Mere presidential or independent campaigning is thus not equivalent to populism.

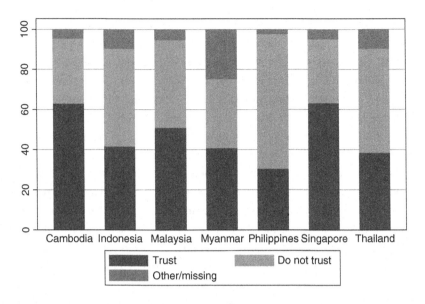

Figure 1 Trust in Parties in Southeast Asia
Source: Asian Barometer Waves 3 (Indonesia) and 4 (all others)

deeply institutionalized memberships, that populists thrive. For this reason, populism has been historically far more successful in Southeast Asia and Latin America than in Western Europe, at least until recent years (Kenny 2017).

Clientelistic party systems, such as those that have prevailed in Southeast Asia, have persistently been weaker and more susceptible to appeals by populists than bureaucratic ones. Between 1980 and 2010, worldwide, there were no cases of a populist winning sole executive control in a non-clientelistic party system (Kenny 2017: 188–189). In turn, however, some clientelistic party systems have been weaker and more susceptible to populist appeals than others. Clientelistic party systems in which the central leadership can maintain tight control over the distribution of patronage, such as the Liberal Democratic Party (LDP) did in Japan for many years, can be enduring and resistant to populism. Where clientelism goes in tandem with the extensive autonomy of lower-level political intermediaries, parties tend to be weaker and such systems tend to more susceptible to populist appeals (Kenny 2017: 48–56). Explaining the success of populists in Southeast Asia, as elsewhere, requires understanding why the populace has not been incorporated into nationally cohesive bureaucratic parties on the one hand and why the clientelistic parties that did develop have been relatively fragmented (rather than centralized) on the other.

Country specialists will rightly argue that the reasons for the development of the mostly weak and factionalized clientelistic party systems in the region are unique to each case. However, we can identify some general patterns that apply across Southeast Asia. The proximate explanation is the political fragmentation that was built into these polities' systems at the time of their incorporation as modern states, and the acceleration of this process under periods of democratization and decentralization. The deeper explanation concerns the nature of political economic development in the region, which has led to the empowerment of elites who profit from their dominance over government at the subnational level.

These two factors – institutional and political-economic – explain why, on the one hand, bureaucratic national parties have been almost non-existent in democratic Southeast Asia; and why, on the other, clientelistic parties in the region have largely failed to form dominant and enduring national party machines. With the exception of the Communist movements of the 1930s to 1970s, and arguably some contemporary Islamic and ethnic political organizations, most parties in Southeast Asia have been clientelistic rather than bureaucratic. Citizens across the region are typically tied to political parties not via autonomous civil society organizations (e.g., labor unions, churches, nationalist associations), but through ties of patronage to locally prominent individual politicians and their political networks (Aspinall, Davidson et al. 2016, 2015, Hutchcroft 2014, Lande 1968, Scott 1972). Critically also, political loyalties have traditionally taken on a regional or local basis, making these national clientelistic parties particularly fragile. Even national patronage-based parties in the region are better understood as agglomerations of locally oriented networks of patrons and clients (Hicken 2006b). In Indonesia, the Philippines, and Myanmar local autonomy was built into the very nature of the colonial state. In Thailand, although never a formal colony and although bureaucratic centralization has been the stated rule, political party penetration in the local arena has always been shallow. Party institutionalization has been notoriously weak in the region, even in its most durable democracy, the Philippines (Hicken and Kuhonta 2014).[2]

In practice, local elites in the region, whether as landlords, employers, providers of credit, or later, government agents, were able to convert their local predominance into political power, effectively staving off political

---

[2] The United Malays National Organisation (UMNO) in Malaysia and the People's Action Party (PAP) in Singapore are partial exceptions to this general rule. Both UMNO and especially PAP, like the LDP in Japan, developed as relatively more institutionalized and centralized machine parties that also cultivated links with religious and ethnic associations through the distribution of patronage (Weiss and Hassan 2003).

centralization and effective national party building as imperial influence waned in the middle of the twentieth century. Vote buying became prevalent across the region as democracy was introduced but these transactions did not generate enduring political loyalties. The growing importance of natural resources, from crude oil to palm oil, only increased the dependence of the economic elite on political connections and control over the enforcement of the law. Right from independence, weakly institutionalized national parties were formed, challenged, or captured by leaders with at least some populist characteristics: Sukarno in Indonesia, Ramon Magsaysay and Ferdinand Marcos in the Philippines, and Tunku Abdul Rahman in Malaysia. The same probably would have been true of Aung San in Burma, had he lived, and was arguably true of U Nu in the latter part of his rule.

Across the region, long periods of authoritarian centralism emerged partly as a response to the political and economic fragmentation of the early post-independence period (Slater 2010). Yet, with the exception of the People's Action Party (PAP) in Singapore, and to a lesser extent the United Malays National Organization (UMNO) in Malaysia, bureaucratic parties failed to develop out of this restriction of the political space. Even in Indonesia, where Golkar, the party apparatus of the ruling Suharto regime, became a national party through its considerable presence in the burgeoning administrative machinery across the country, the party continued to be weakly embedded in society, while other parties were prohibited entirely from having a presence below the regency level (Tan 2012: 83). In Timor-Leste, the *Frente Revolucionaria de Timor-Leste Independente* (FRETILIN), which was the party most associated with winning independence, had the potential to entrench itself as a nationally representative bureaucratic party; however, it lost power after just a single term in government as voters abandoned it for a multitude of new alternatives (Hynd 2017). In Thailand, even a decade after the democratic transition of 1993, parties still had only a shallow penetration into large parts of the country, with local notables and factions having extensive influence (Ockey 2003).

In a deeper sense, the subnational political fragmentation of the region is due in part to its political economy. The concentration of elite capital in primary industries – plantation production and minerals among others – meant that there was little by way of an industrial elite centralizing counterweight to locally entrenched plutocrats as has existed in northeast Asia in more recent times (Robison 1986). As historical research on Europe and North America shows, such modern business groups played a key role in the consolidation of programmatic parties (Kuo 2018). In contrast, Southeast Asian elites, dependent on local monopolies for rents and the use of coercion to extract economic surpluses from workers and peasants, have been best served by a system in which they retained effective political control. Rapid growth in recent decades has done little to alter this entrenched system, as powerful elites have the capacity to resist encroachment on their prerogatives (Winters 2011), while urban populations are fragmented by cross-cutting work status, class, ethnic, and religious cleavages.

The persistent weakness of national parties – both bureaucratic and clientelistic – has meant that the transitions to democracy in Southeast Asia beginning in the 1980s have been accompanied by the recurrent presence of populist campaigners who have relied on their charismatic appeal to link directly with voters without the baggage of densely institutionalized parties. Just as Corazon "Cory" Aquino, Joseph Estrada, and Susilo Bambang Yudhoyono challenged and defeated non-populist parties in the Philippines and Indonesia when they re-democratized in the 1980s and 1990s respectively, Thaksin Shinawatra came to power in Thailand through direct appeals to voters who were only weakly attached – if at all – to establishment non-populist national parties. In Timor-Leste, FRETILIN held power for just one term before losing to a coalition led by Xanana Gusmão's populist electoral vehicle, the *Congresso Nacional da Reconstrucao Timorense* (CNRT), in 2007. The National League for Democracy's (NLD) thumping victory in the 2015 parliamentary elections in Myanmar would have been inconceivable without the charismatic Aung San Suu Kyi at its helm on the one hand and the institutional weakness of the military-established Union Solidarity and Development Party (USDP) on the other. Populism, rather than representing something extraordinary, has been nearly ever-present in democratic Southeast Asia, existing in continual tension with clientelistic forms of party building (c.f., Hellmann 2017). At times the latter has been sufficient to produce ruling national coalitions, but these have rarely lasted more than one or two electoral cycles before being threatened or overturned by populist competitors.

Political theorists have long argued that populists paradoxically pose a threat to the very democratic institutions that allow them to come to power. In seeking to establish and maintain a *direct* relationship to supporters, populists are inherently driven to erode the intermediary institutions that might get in the way (Urbinati 2015); this includes parties, courts, legislatures, the press, the academy, or any other agency that purports to challenge the populist's singular legitimacy. A growing body of empirical research now demonstrates that populists erode democracy across most measurable dimensions (Allred, Hawkins et al. 2015, Houle and Kenny 2018, Huber and Schimpf 2016, Kenny 2017: ch. 2, Kenny 2018, Ruth 2018). Liberal democracy seems to work only when coherent bureaucratic political parties exist to manage it.

Is this antagonistic relationship evident in Southeast Asia? On the one hand, populists such as Thaksin and Duterte have so eroded *liberal* procedures such as press freedom and the rule of law that their democratic credentials are in serious doubt. Other populists, however, such as Yudhoyono and Jokowi in Indonesia and Xanana Gusmão in Timor-Leste, even if they are best classified as *partial* populists (who were partly constrained by their legislative coalition partners), have been much more moderate. Moreover, non-populist governments in Southeast Asia, whether authoritarian or democratic have been frequent abusers of civil rights. Populist government in Thailand, for example, was ultimately curtailed by military intervention, which in turn resulted in even more severe repression of freedom of speech and other civil liberties. Given the frequency of coups in Thailand, it is hard to argue that this was a response to Thaksin's alleged abuses alone. Military rule in Indonesia and Myanmar has been savagely violent. Rather than populism being simply a "threat" to democracy, it seems that the perennial weakness of political parties in Southeast Asia sets up a recurrent three-way tension between populism, clientelistic democracy, and authoritarianism. The kinds of civil rights taken for granted in Western democracies have been weakly upheld by all types of government in the region. Populism is thus as much a symptom as a cause of weak democracy and weak parties in the region.

Section 2 develops the organizational conceptualization of populism. Section 3 discusses existing explanations for the prevalence of populism in the region and adds flesh to the theoretical framework introduced in Section 1. Section 4 outlines the historical political economic and institutional basis for the weakness of national parties in the region and Section 5 details how populists have taken advantage of this to appeal directly to voters in the Philippines, Indonesia, and Thailand. Section 6 concludes with some thoughts on what we can learn from these cases on the relationship between populism and democracy.

2 Defining Populism

Populism is a term used with such frequency in both academic and non-academic writing that its meaning can be difficult to fix. By almost any measure, populists are a diverse group with seemingly few shared commitments or characteristics. It has thus been a considerable challenge to develop a concept that has a consistent theoretical core and that adequately categorizes those groups classified as populist in ordinary language. Populism literally means "a practice, system, or doctrine of the people." How exactly this people-centric form of politics should be conceived of and operationalized remains an open question.

There are (at least) two major schools of thought on conceptualizing and operationalizing populism (for a thorough recent review, see Moffitt 2016). I call these the *ideational* and *organizational* approaches.[3] This Element builds on the organizational approach used in the early wave of political sociological studies of populism in Latin America (Di Tella 1965, Germani 1978, Mouzelis 1985, van Niekerk 1974), developed by Weyland (2001, 2017), and most recently operationalized by Kenny (2017). Populist movements or parties can be distinguished from both bureaucratic and clientelistic organizations based on how they are structured internally and how they mobilize support externally (Kenny 2017). In this sense, populism can be understood as *the charismatic mobilization of a mass movement in pursuit of political power.*

The key distinguishing feature of populism in this formulation is charismatic mobilization. I follow Max Weber's (1978: 1111–1114) well-known tripartite distinction between bureaucratic, patrimonial, and charismatic forms of authority. The exercise of authority within bureaucratic parties is bound by rules and procedures, while externally they are founded on stable institutionalized relationships with supporters (Panebianco 1988, Sartori 1976). Analogously, in patrimonial organizations, authority is both traditional and transactional. Leadership is often inherited and privileges are distributed to supporters in return for their loyalty. Externally, such patronage-based parties engage in a quid pro quo with supporters in which votes are exchanged for particularistic material benefits (Eisenstadt and Roniger 1980, Hicken 2011, Scott 1972, Stokes, Dunning et al. 2013). Charismatic authority is instead characterized by the concentration of arbitrary control in the person of a popularly acclaimed leader.

While this tripartite schema – bureaucratic, clientelistic, and populist – resembles that of Kitschelt's (2000) party typology, our understandings of "bureaucratic" or "programmatic" party linkages differ. Thus, for clarity in this Element, I generally use Weber's original, but less familiar, terminology of the *bureaucratic* party rather than that of the programmatic party, although I take the two to be synonymous (see Kenny 2017). In contrast to Kitschelt (2000), bureaucratic (or programmatic) parties are not defined herein by their association with a particular ideology or set of policies. Parties of all types, not least populist ones, frequently make policy-based (or programmatic in Kitschelt's sense) appeals to voters (Barr 2009). One of the novel contributions

---

[3] This Element's focus on organizations and strategies is not to suggest that the rhetoric or policy positions of populist actors do not matter. On the contrary, they matter a great deal. They are the *means* by which populist actors mobilize electoral support. However, the "anti-establishment" or "anti-elite" discourse that is so common to such actors is, I argue, endogenous to how their movements are *organized* (Kenny 2017: 24-28).

of the organizational conceptualization of populism advanced here is the idea that policy-based appeals are in fact an important part of what populists do. As scholars in the *ideational* school have long recognized, populism often combines with other *host* ideologies (Mudde and Rovira Kaltwasser 2018: 4). In turn, following Weber (1978), bureaucratic or programmatic parties are defined by the institutionalization of their internal management and external relationships with supporters. It is a description of how they are organized rather than of the messages or policies they advocate.

Charismatic authority is defined by the situating of authority within the arbitrary control of the leader. Charismatic leadership is often thought to be a description of a leader's character. It would seem, in this sense, to have little relation to "the people." However, Weber (1978) was in fact clear that the distinctive element of charismatic authority was that it depends not on rules or tradition but on popular acclamation. For Weber (1978), a leader is charismatic only to the extent that his followers treat him as such. As he put it, "It is recognition on the part of those subject to authority which is decisive for the validity of charisma" (242). Charisma, in other words, is "an attribute of the belief of the followers and not of the quality of the leader" (Bensman and Givant 1975: 578). Charismatic leadership thus describes a relationship or a type of formal or informal organization, not a set of character traits.

Even more than for bureaucratic or patrimonial organizations, the people are the key actors in understanding how charisma works in practice. Weber (1978: 1114–1115) writes, the "genuinely charismatic ruler" is "responsible to the ruled – responsible, that is, to prove that he himself is indeed the master willed by God . . . If the people withdraw their recognition, the master becomes a mere private person." It is the fact that supporters can withdraw their support that makes the charismatic leadership of the masses a people-centric form of politics. Mere charismatic leadership, it should be noted, however, is not the same thing as populism. To the extent that charismatic leadership is possible in more conspiratorial form – think of Hitler's Nazi Party of the early 1920s or Lenin's Bolshevik faction prior to the First World War – we have to draw a further contrast between mere charismatic leadership and populism. A large mass of the people is critical to populism in a way that is distinct from charismatic leadership per se. Hence populism refers to the charismatic mobiliation of a *mass* movement.

Populists seek to connect *directly*, figuratively if not literally, with the masses who become their *supporters*. Supporters are mobilized less by clientelistic ties or membership in aligned parties or civil society organizations than they are by a direct *affinity for the leader* (Weyland 2001: 14, Wiles 1969: 167). Although populists sometimes utilize parties, unions, and other organizations in their efforts to win and retain power, they rely more on ad hoc, leader-centric, and weakly institutionalized organizational structures composed of devoted *followers* than on the persistent formal and informal institutions of bureaucratic or clientelistic parties. However, populism is not simply a synonym for presidential mobilization in weak party systems or for independent campaigning more generally.

Populists lead mass *movements* in the sense that followers develop an affinity for a collective project (itself, however, ill-defined) that is identified with a leader (Hoffer 1951). That project, as ideational theorists have argued, can take the form of opposition to the establishment, elites, minorities, criminals, or immigrants. Critical from the organizational perspective, however, is that this project takes a distinct institutional form. Charismatic leaders drive, as well as divine, the popular will. Drawing wide boundaries around a potential support base (by excluding elites and minorities from the people) and tapping into, if not creating, a movement with some sense of purpose makes sense as a mobilization strategy for the leader of a party that lacks societal depth. Mass movements are characterized by the use of repertoires of constituency-making contention, whether this means attending political rallies, following a dress code, or simply the consumption and distribution of social media content (Tilly and Wood 2013). Mass belief in a leader's charisma often comes in the wake of the conversion of a core of true believers or followers of a movement who in turn evangelize in *His* name. Such movements can be relatively amorphous, with porous and ephemeral memberships, but the point to stress is that populism is by no means inimical to organization, as some critics of the organizational approach have assumed.[4] What is critical is that populist leaders are not constrained by organizational rules and have total authority over personnel and strategic decisions within their movement, organization, or party. This is not true of independent, personalist, or presidentialist movements per se. Populist movements may take the form of a party but do not have to. In places like Indonesia and the Philippines, parties are legally obligated when it comes to nominating a candidate for the presidency. In other places around the world, looser movements are possible. Whether they are parties or movements, however, authority is arbitrary and concentrated in the person of the leader.

Charismatic leaders do sometimes rely on material inducements and party and civil society organizations to mobilize voters. For instance, in Indonesia, even the most quintessential of charismatic campaigners, Prabowo Subianto, felt compelled to distribute cash and other gifts to voters; these gifts do not guarantee a vote, but may be an "entry ticket" required of any candidate with hopes of winning an election (Aspinall 2015, Aspinall, Michael Davidson et al. 2015). While the targets

---

[4] Note the subtle but important departure from Weyland (2001).

of populist mobilization are likely to be unattached or swing voters, this is not a defining feature of populism, but a tendency that varies from one context to another in its intensity. Indeed, as research elsewhere has shown, voters may be embedded in party patronage networks at the local level, while still supporting a populist at the national level (Kenny 2017). Charismatic leaders also make policy-based and identity-based appeals, as I describe further below. The difference between populist and non-populist leaders falls on the charismatic organizational dimension, both with respect to internal control over a leader's movement (or party) and with respect to his or her external relationship with supporters (the masses). A leader is populist to the *degree* that he or she relies primarily on the charismatic mobilization of a mass movement (Weyland 2017).

The critical questions we need to ask with respect to the internal dimension are: Is the movement or party one that the leader formed as a personal electoral vehicle? Is authority within the leader's party or movement arbitrary – completely at the discretion of the leader – or rule based? Does the leader control appointment decisions or is leadership/appointment determined by ballot or some other collective procedure? The critical questions to ask with respect to the external dimension are: Does the leader's movement or party rely primarily on mass rallies, mass media, and social media to mobilize electoral support directly, or does it rely primarily on mobilizing voters through unions, churches, or other organizations or on systematic clientelism? Is the leader himself/herself the primary object of a campaign or is it a party's historical political/group/ethnic linkages to a constituency? Based on the degree to which leaders meet these criteria, we can distinguish between *partial* and *full* populists, with the caveat that *full* is an ideal type that is rarely reached in practice. Section 3 theorizes the conditions under which populists in this sense are more or less successful. Section 4 details the historical development of those conditions in Southeast Asia's three major contemporary democracies – the Philippines, Indonesia, and Thailand – and Section 5 examines how populists have exploited these conditions to mobilize support in those countries since the return of democracy beginning in the 1980s.

3 The Causes of Populism in Southeast Asia

Although individual cases of populist success in Southeast Asia have been analyzed in various books and articles, there have been few efforts to develop a more general model of populist success in the region. Most of the general theories of populist success come from the differing experiences of Western Europe and Latin America. In this section, I first review these various theories before presenting an alternative.

Explaining Populist Success in Southeast Asia

Until recently, the predominant approach to understanding populism has been to focus on the type(s) of macro-level social and economic conditions in which populists supposedly thrive. Indeed, this was the approach of the earliest systematic academic treatment of the subject (Ionescu and Gellner 1969) and is the approach followed in this Element. This general approach has taken two broad forms. The first has been to look toward long-term macro-structural developments such as economic modernization. The second has been to concentrate on more proximate challenges to the political status quo such as economic and security crises. These conditions are said to create the "demand" for anti-establishment candidates who are not tarnished by a record of incompetence or corruption in government. Recent research has begun to explore the micro-foundations of populist support, but, as I explain further below, we still lack a general theory for variation in support for populism at the individual level.

A number of authors have argued that populists, especially in Western Europe, have gained at the expense of non-populist parties because the latter have moved away from the interests of their supporters. In particular, in response to the structural economic crises of the 1970s, social democratic parties are alleged to have abandoned their traditional support for full employment and the welfare state, thus losing the backing of their traditional working-class supporters. This in turn has led to a rise of a distinct brand of populism that combines hostility toward immigrants with a return to the post-war welfare state, or a kind of welfare chauvinism (Bornschier 2010, Judis 2016, Mouffe 2005). Analogously, scholars have argued that the embrace of neoliberalism in Latin America broke the long-standing ideological linkages between parties, especially labor parties, and voters (Lupu 2016, Roberts 2014a). Although this model of ideological party-system dealignment makes some sense for Western Europe, where partisan political cleavages along economic policy were relatively clear and stable (Bornschier 2010), this logic is problematic in most Southeast Asian (or Latin American) cases, where mainstream parties typically have been indistinguishable in policy terms. That is, ideological dealignment theory can arguably work where prior ideological alignments are themselves clear. However, even in such circumstances, this approach probably overstates the ideological congruence between parties and voters (Kinder and Kalmoe 2017). In fact, to the extent that party supporters share the ideologies of party leaders, it could be that supporting a party causes people to adopt the party's policies and worldviews as their own (Achen and Bartels 2016, Cohen 2003).

However, in a slightly different formulation, the dealignment theory offers some useful insights. Dealignment in this alternative sense is more of a social than an ideological process. Some of the original models of populist success in Latin America looked to deep structural changes in society and the economy to explain the decline of establishment parties and the emergence of populist alternatives. This latter body of research put the focus on how socioeconomic modernization, and attendant processes such as rural–urban migration, broke down old coalitions of voters and created new ones (Germani 1978). These processes of modernization and urbanization disrupted the networks of patronage-based parties and made the success of populist mobilizers such as Juan Perón in Argentina more likely (Collier and Collier 2002). We can see elements of this dynamic playing out across contemporary developing Asia (Berenschot 2010, Swamy 2013). Problematically, however, there is no a priori reason that new groups such as migrants or an inchoate industrial working class cannot be incorporated into existing patronage-based party systems. We thus need an explanation for why these groups do not become attached to extant or new patronage-based parties but gravitate toward populist ones instead.

A number of authors have argued – specifically with reference to Southeast Asia – that it is the structural economic exclusion of the urban proletariat and other groups that has given rise to populist mobilization (Swamy 2013, Thompson 2016b). Case (2017), for example, argues that populist mobilization in Southeast Asia is precipitated by intra-elite splits in the presence of favorable social coalitions. That is, particular elites look to exploit available social coalitions through populist appeals in order to gain dominance over their rivals. While this approach rightly incorporates the office-seeking goals of political elites, its treatment of the structural opportunities that make populist mobilization successful is problematic. In particular, the exact nature of these coalitions of marginalized groups remains murky. Hadiz (2016: 28) applies this line of reasoning to the rise of so-called Islamic populist movements and offers some more clarity. He argues that Islamic movements have sought to unite a sociologically diverse coalition of "upwardly mobile members of the middle class, excluded members of entrepreneurial groups and downtrodden members of the lumpenproletariat," in opposition to the ruling secular elite. Yet not all populists operate in this way. Indeed, survey evidence from the Philippines indicates that Duterte's support comes not just from the "left behind" or struggling middle classes but also from the well to do.[5] The diversity of populists' support

---

[5] Jasmine Punzala, "Duterte woos more believers in NCR, class ABC: survey," *News ABC-CBN*, April 25, 2016, http://news.abs-cbn.com/halalan2016/nation/04/25/16/duterte-woos-more-believers-in-ncr-class-abc-survey, accessed July 31, 2018.

bases makes any attempt to explain the success of populist movements as a direct result of underlying class cleavages problematic.

A possible resolution to this problem turns on the role of identity. Perhaps one of the few consistent characteristics of populists is that they claim – explicitly or implicitly – to represent the people (Canovan 1999, Mudde 2004). The people might be conceived of in nationalist, religious, ethnic, or other terms. Populist mobilization in these cases thus might be interpreted as a response to challenges to a political community defined in terms of a particular identity. In Europe, this has often manifested itself as the opposition of "native" populations against non-European (especially Muslim) immigrants; in the United States, resurgent white nationalist sentiment opposes both Latino immigrants and African Americans; in Southeast Asia, such identity-based mobilization has typically been drawn along the lines of domestic majority-minority ethnoreligious cleavages. In Indonesia, for example, Chinese and Christian minorities have been the subjects of prejudice at the hands of fundamentalist or scripturalist Muslims (Hadiz 2016). Mietzner (2018: 264) persuasively argues that the Islamist "mass movement" of 2016 under the leadership of Rizieq Shibab should be understood as a case of populism. However, the electoral success of populist candidates and parties in this context is highly dependent on the strategic behavior of establishment parties, making it indeterminate as a theory. We have no good structural theory to explain why establishment parties choose to resist or embrace anti-immigrant or anti-minority mobilization. Ethnonationalist or religious platforms are possible without populist mobilization (Mietzner and Muhtadi 2018), so the presence of such cleavages alone does not explain the success of populist movements per se.[6]

Another approach to this question has been to focus on populism as a set of individual attitudes that cuts across typical economic interests and sociocultural identities. Taking the view that populists offer a distinctive ideological platform that is pro-people, anti-elite, and Manichean, scholars have posited that populist parties are successful because they tap into widely held "populist" sentiments (Hawkins and Rovira Kaltwasser 2018). This approach follows the predominant spatial logic used to explain political behavior in industrialized democracies, but instead of the political space being divided along a left-right (economic) dimension, it is divided on a populist–non-populist one (Inglehart and Norris 2017, Krastev 2007). Voters with so-called populist attitudes should support populist candidates. Although intuitive on a theoretical level, the evidence is mixed; some research supports it (Akkerman, Mudde et al. 2013,

---

[6] The United Malay National Organisation (UMNO) and the Malaysian Islamic Party (PAS) provide good examples of non-populist ethno-religious political mobilization.

Bakker, Rooduijn et al. 2016, Dustmann, Eichengreen et al. 2017), while other research does not (Kenny and Holmes 2018, Stanley 2011).

Within Southeast Asia, although more survey data will become available in the near future, at present we only have individual-level populist attitudes for the Philippines. In that case, although the extent of populist attitudes is roughly in line with other non-Western populations, there is little evidence of a direct relationship between populist attitudes as typically measured and approval of (or trust in) Rodrigo Duterte, a prototypical populist leader (Kenny and Holmes 2018). It should be noted, however, that these attitudes are strongly associated with distinct policy preferences. At present, although this line of research holds some promise, we do not have a satisfactory model or set of models for why populist attitudes are activated in some cases, and for some individuals, but not others.

Another barrier to this line of inquiry, at least in the short term, is that even if there is an empirical relationship between populist attitudes and support for populists, we lack the kinds of dynamic data that are needed to disentangle the social psychological processes behind it. That is, we just don't yet know whether the relationship between populist attitudes and political behavior is causal or in which direction the effect might go. What if, in other words, support for a populist leader makes individuals more likely to hold so-called populist views (Rooduijn, van der Brug et al. 2016)? This might sound like hair splitting, but establishing the direction of the causal arrow is critical. Just as research on party identification and ideology in the United States has found that people often change their ideology or policy preferences to fit with that of their party (Achen and Bartels 2016, Cohen 2003), it could be that people like a populist candidate for some idiosyncratic reason and then subsequently come to adopt his or her worldview as their own. Populist attitudes may also be unstable. In the Philippines, for example, Kenny and Holmes (2018) show that populist attitudes in the population increased after a year of Dutere rule, although because they do not have panel data, we cannot tell if attitudes changed at the individual level. Understanding voter preferences remains a vital area of future research but until we have more systematic panel and experimental data to answer these questions at a psychological level, the more appropriate question remains the sociological one: what socioeconomic and political conditions make successful populist mobilization more likely?

One of the best-developed areas of research on populism focuses on the economy. The theory runs that voters abandon established parties for populist alternatives following acute economic crises. A downward turn in the business cycle negatively affects the popularity of existing parties especially in lower- and middle-income countries, where states are unable to adequately compensate for slowdowns in the private sector and basic livelihoods are threatened (Weyland 2006). Under such conditions, populist opposition to existing institutional arrangements attains widespread appeal. In Southeast Asia, for example, both Thaksin and Estrada came to power after periods of deep economic crisis (De Castro 2007).

However, the relationship between economic crisis and populist success has significant empirical shortcomings. First, in cases like the ones just noted, the proximity of the downturn to the electoral success of a populist campaigner varies widely. The Philippines was right in the middle of the 1997–1998 Asian financial crisis when Estrada won power; Thailand, in contrast, was already recovering by the time that Thaksin was elected in 2001. It is thus unclear what kind of lag between economic downturn and populist success should be expected. Second, selecting on cases in which populists are successful fails to take into account the many instances in which severe and sustained economic crises did not lead to the embrace of populist candidates. It also fails to explain why populists such as Yudhoyono or Duterte would have come to power under benign economic conditions. In Duterte's case, the economy of the Philippines was experiencing a sustained economic expansion prior to his election. In previous quantitative studies of a larger number of cases, no correlation between economic crisis and populist success emerges (Doyle 2011, Kenny 2017).

Finally, some scholars have argued that electoral laws are an important intervening mechanism if not an alternative explanation in their own right. Presidential systems or other electoral rules such as the personal vote may result in weaker parties (Hicken 2009). However, it is often problematical to treat these institutions as exogenous causes of party strength (Boix 1999), as in part they reflect the preferences of the political elites who introduce them. Perhaps only in the unusual case of Indonesia, where open party lists were introduced as a result of a Constitutional Court ruling, might such institutions be treated as exogenous (Kenny 2017: 146). In any case, even in parliamentary systems such as Thailand or semi-presidential ones like Timor-Leste, contrary to this institutional logic, aspiring candidates can effectively build parties on the fly. In such cases, if the individual characteristics of the leader are sufficiently important to voters, many parliamentarians are willing to defect to the side of the most popular candidate (either before or after an election). In cases such as Indonesia, where any presidential candidate must be nominated by a party or coalition of parties with a minimum representation in the legislature, the opportunity for outsider candidates is more limited. Yet even there populists like Yudhoyono and Prabowo have been able to create their own electoral vehicles, or take over existing ones, and ride them into power (or close to it). Thus, electoral rules seem to play only a minor role in explaining populist success.

Fragmentation and Populism: Explaining Party Weakness and Populist Strength

What is missing in these various theories is a coherent model of why non-populist parties have only weak and contingent ties to voters and why populism is the specific response to that weakness. The underlying configurations of party–voter linkage make a polity more or less vulnerable to populist mobilization. At some times and places these linkages are stable while at others they are not. Elsewhere I argue that different types of party–voter linkage are established and decay in different ways (Kenny 2017). In Southeast Asia, bureaucratic party–voter linkages have been relatively uncommon, with only Communist and some identity-based parties adopting this type of institutional linkage with their supporters. Thus, models that focus on ideological party system dealignment have limited applicability to the region. The main forms of linkage in Southeast Asia have been clientelistic and authoritarian, with populist linkages emerging as a frequent challenger to them.

In clientelistic party systems, the way in which patronage networks are organized plays a critical role in system stability. Not all patronage-based party systems are as susceptible to populist opposition. I argue that more decentralized or fragmented patronage-based systems are vulnerable to populist outflanking, while more centralized patronage-based systems are more stable and more resistant to populist challenges (Kenny 2017). In patronage-based or clientelistic party systems, political parties are linked with supporters by the distribution of patronage through a network of subnational *brokers*. Brokers receive the patronage of political leaders at the national level in return for mobilizing vote banks from below; broker loyalty is thus a key problem for the durability of patronage-based parties (Aspinall 2014b, Novaes 2018, Stokes, Dunning et al. 2013). While such systems theoretically operate as an integrated machine, brokers often have both the incentive and the capacity to "betray" their patrons (Aspinall 2014b).

Drawing on principal agent theory and social network theory, I argue that greater broker autonomy in patronage democracies is associated with weaker ties between *national* parties and voters, which makes the latter available for direct mobilization by populists (Kenny 2017: 48–56). Where brokers at the subnational level have significant autonomy from party leaderships at the center, they can reap nearly all of the political capital earned by the distribution of patronage, even if they do not ensure that their clients vote for associated national parties or candidates in higher-level elections. Under such circumstances, local brokers have little incentive to systematically deliver votes to the national party leadership. For their part, voters receive the benefits of patronage from their local brokers irrespective of who is in power at the national level. Voters may thus feel little obligation to choose candidates from the same party at different levels of government. This leaves the national-level units of parties unattached to voters directly and vulnerable to the self-interested behavior of brokers (Aspinall, Davidson et al. 2016). Thus, unlike in a centrally controlled patronage party system, voters are under little or no compulsion to choose a national party on the basis of whether or not it will provide them with patronage. Voters may choose the party or candidate endorsed by their local broker, but the *probability* that they will choose a candidate based on his or her *charismatic leadership* is therefore increased when brokers are more autonomous.

However, the mere fact that non-populist national parties have weak connections with voters creates the *opportunity* for populist outflanking does not guarantee that it will occur or that it will be successful. To understand why populism is so often a successful strategy in these cases, we need to consider the difficulty faced by alternatives and the particular resources and strategies that populists by definition can employ.

First, the specific configuration of patronage-based party systems makes populist mobilization a much more likely outcome than the emergence of a bureaucratic party rival. Because in patronage democracies political ties take the form of vertically integrated patron–client factions, movements based on broad-based national organizations (e.g., Labor unions) are more difficult (though of course not impossible) to form. That is, society is already organized into vertical silos of patrons and clients or into regional or identity-based patronage machines (Chandra 2004), preventing the formation of the kind of broad-based organizations that underlay the consolidation of the bureaucratic labor and social democratic parties of early twentieth century Europe. As the latter kinds of case illustrate, bureaucratic parties take a long time to develop. Moreover, the development of such parties, and the kinds of conservative parties that developed to compete with them, may be historically contingent (Kuo 2018, Ziblatt 2017). The different technologies of mass production, war fighting, and social interaction that existed a hundred years ago may have made such parties possible in a way that is no longer the case in contemporary Southeast Asia.

Second, populists' use of public appearances, mass rallies, the traditional mass media, and increasingly social media makes for a relatively *low cost* means of connecting with masses of voters. Of course, all political parties use such tactics to a degree. The difference is that populists rely *primarily* on these direct connections rather than party members, sympathizers, or paid brokers to deliver votes for them. Critically, this lowers the *entry cost* of populist mobilization when compared to other types of mobilization. Populist appeals may or may not include explicit reference to "the people." Critically, however, they are organizationally based on direct appeals to broad constituencies that are relatively unattached to (or at least easily detachable from) parties at the national level. Unlike the leaders of patronage parties, populists don't need a nationwide system of brokers to mobilize votes. Analogously, unlike bureaucratic parties, populists don't need the deeply institutionalized links with supporters through interest groups and other civil society organizations that take many years to build. A single charismatic candidate like a Prabowo Subianto or a Joseph Estrada can utilize their personal connections or extant celebrity to build a position in the polls. In particularly weak party systems, voter choice often comes down to the trustworthiness of the individual candidate. Here populists' outsider status confers a distinct advantage, while being a "party man" can be a disadvantage. Even partial populist candidates like Jokowi, who come from mainstream clientelist parties, often pitch themselves as standing independent of the party machinery and against the "establishment."

Third, contrary to the idea that the supporters of populists are not motivated by policy while the supporters of bureaucratic parties are, this framework posits that policy appeals may be highly relevant to populist voters. Because populists are not institutionally tied to clear interests groups, it is often the case that their messaging is vague on policy specifics, especially on the economy. As Prime Minister of Thailand, Thaksin said, "I'm applying socialism in the lower economy and capitalism in the upper economy" (quoted in Wilkin 2018: 27–28). However, on certain issues, populists look to draw cleavages in which they appeal to very large majorities of the people. They oppose crime, corruption, immigrants, religious minorities, or sometimes the oligarchy, thus drawing very capacious boundaries around their potential support group. At the micro-level, supporters of populists may be attracted by these policy appeals (Kenny and Holmes 2018). However, this does not make populist movements "bureaucratic" (or "programmatic" in the Weberian sense). It is not policy that divides populist and non-populist candidates or parties but organization. Ironically, in fact, given the enduring nature of their party loyalties, it could be that the supporters of bureaucratic parties are less motivated by policy than the supporters of populists (Green, Palmquist et al. 2002).

However, even if attracted to a populist candidate in part because of a particular policy, trust – or "faith" as Weber (1978) put it – in the ability of that particular leader to deliver on such policies is also critical for populist supporters. We don't yet understand the psychological processes behind the belief in a given leader's charisma (Kenny and Holmes 2018). The research that exists suggests that the ability to continue performing extraordinary feats of governance seems to be important in maintaining charismatic authority (Willner 1984). Thus, while the supporters of bureaucratic parties remain loyal even as policies and performance vary (Green, Palmquist et al. 2002), support for populists remains contingent on performance (or at least on *perceptions* of performance) unless it can be institutionalized (e.g., made clientelistic in the mode of Juan Perón's Justicalist Party in Argentina). This logic accounts for the widely observed tendency for populists to constrain democracy once in power (Houle and Kenny 2018, Kenny 2017: 39–46).

In sum, populism thrives as an efficient (low cost) form of political mobilization where bureaucratic and *centralized* clientelistic party building are inhibited. The only credible alternatives in such circumstances are looser and contingent patronage-based networks or coalitions, or, as has frequently happened, authoritarianism. While this model travels well to Southeast Asia, a number of questions arise: What explains the origins of these fragmented patronage-based political structures? If broker autonomy is detrimental to the formation of strong national parties, why have central political elites not prevented it, especially given the long periods of authoritarian rule in each of these cases that might have allowed for such top-down institutional engineering?

These questions force us to look to the deeper political economic roots of party systems (Lipset and Rokkan 1967). Trivially, we can say that political systems in democracies should reflect the balance of social, economic, and political power in a society (Boix 1999, Cusack, Iversen et al. 2007). For example, if landlords and other elites dependent on the primary sector largely control the economy, the justice system, and the prevailing social order, we would expect any political party system to be a reflection of their interests. This might mean property requirements to participate in politics, overrepresentation of rural areas, and the decentralization of fiscal policy and judicial authority to the local level. Such arrangements in turn facilitate incorporation through vertical ties of patronage. In contrast, if industrialists contribute the greater share of economic production, employ the most workers, and control the public sphere (e.g., media), the party system should be more nationalized and centralized, with greater representation of urban areas, and so on (Caramani 2004). At the same time, a more industrialized economy should go hand-in-hand with greater opportunities for labor to organize and gain political representation (Rueschemeyer, Huber et al. 1992); for their part, conservative (landholding) interests need to establish cross-class coalitions of supporters utilizing other networks such as churches (Ziblatt 2017). In short, the more industrialized an economy, the more *likely* party voter linkages are to be bureaucratic (Kuo 2018, Stokes, Dunning et al. 2013: ch. 8). The composition of a country's political economy thus has a significant impact on the system of party–voter linkages and the likelihood of populist mobilization being successful.

Yet the argument put forward here is not economically determinist. We need to be very wary of falling into the trap of a naïve modernization theory paradigm. In each of the senses noted below, path dependency matters. First, there is the possibility of feedback loops. Incumbent elites can advance or stymie the process of industrialization in order to preserve or enhance their power (Wilkin 2018: 136–137, 160–165). The lack of economic modernization may be as much a product as a cause of the power of conservative or administrative elites. Second, mere development is not sufficient to create bureaucratic parties. Once entrenched, patronage-based systems are highly resilient to change (Shefter 1994). This is especially the case under conditions of decentralization where multiple veto players can stymie reform (Kenny 2015b). Third, and relatedly, brokers in a patronage network can owe their local power to a variety of sources: landed wealth, control over a business in a protected sector (e.g. oil, telecoms), or a position in the administration. Mere development is not linearly related to how regulations produce and maintain such veto points (North, Wallis et al. 2012). Finally, key moments of state formation and reformation matter for the distribution of political economic power and for the kinds of political party system that goes with it because they create a window, or critical juncture, during which elites and the masses can renegotiate the terms of political incorporation (Collier and Collier 2002). In some cases, these windows of opportunity result in a radical reformulation of a nation's institutional structure (Kenny 2015a, Kenny 2015b). In Singapore, for instance, decolonization and the threat of domestic insurgency led elites to support the creation of a strong centralized state (Slater 2010). In Indonesia, in contrast, the fall of Suharto's government reawakened strong fissiparous tendencies that lay dormant during the New Order.

This theory generates implications at both the macro- and micro-levels. At the macro-level, we would expect that clientelistic party systems where brokers have extensive autonomy from the central political leadership will be more susceptible to populist appeals as voters are not compelled to choose the same parties at the local and national levels in order to access patronage. At the micro-level, supporters of populists are likely to be motivated by identity or touchstone policy issues (e.g., immigration, corruption, crime), but we would expect variation in support for populist leaders to be most associated with the lack of embeddedness in a national (bureaucratic or clientelistic) party network. Although evidence at the individual level is becoming more widely available, we lack the kind of panel data required for a full-fledged test of these micro-level mechanisms. Thus, while this Element presents some individual-level survey data, empirically it concentrates on the theory's macro-level implications.

In Section 4, I analyze political development in the region, focusing on the Philippines, Indonesia, and Thailand. In these countries, the weakness of national parties has been a result of highly fragmented socioeconomic structures dependent on the primary sector on the one hand, and the creation of political institutions during key moments of state formation in which national and local elites compete for power on the other. In a proximate sense, patronage-based parties in Southeast Asia have been distinctively fragmented due in large part to the centrifugal pressures felt at the end of colonial rule (Kenny 2015b) and democratization during the third (or fourth) wave. More distally, however, this fragmented system of political incorporation, to use Mouzelis's (1985) terminology, is a product of the region's political economy, which itself was largely shaped by its incorporation into the late colonial global economy (Booth 1999, Crouch 1985). As I further describe in Section 4, in each of the Philippines, Indonesia, and Thailand, even several decades of centralizing authoritarian rule did not much alter this fragmented political structure. In Section 5, I turn to the populist response to these conditions.

4 Fragmented Parties

This section examines the history of party development in Southeast Asia with a focus on the Philippines, Indonesia, and Thailand, explaining why, with some exceptions, democratic parties have been so fragmented across the region. Political incorporation in Southeast Asia has largely taken the form of patron–client mobilization (Scott 1972). Due to their local political influence, brokers inhibited the formation of coherent conservative and social democratic parties. Major (mostly non-democratic) Communist movements developed in most countries in Southeast Asia through the mass recruitment of peasants or urban laborers and students. The common response to this combination of political fragmentation and radicalism across the region was authoritarian centralism. Even since the return of democracy to the region from the late 1980s, however, parties have remained weak, and successful populist mobilization has been a relatively frequent outcome.

This section will examine how and why local notables, whether of landed, economic, or administrative origins, became entrenched as the key locus of politics in the Philippines, Indonesia, and Thailand and how they maintained their power and influence through the varying periods of authoritarian rule from the 1960s to the 1990s or regained it quickly thereafter. In Section 5, I look at the rise of populist challengers to that status quo in the 2000s.

The Colonial Origins of Fragmented Clientelism

The Philippines' notoriously fragmented patronage democracy of the post-independence years had its roots in the institutional system put in place first during Spanish colonial rule from the late sixteenth century and consolidated during the decades of American colonial rule beginning at the end of the nineteenth century. The introduction of partially representative institutions early in the twentieth century, prior to the peasant unrest of the interwar period, allowed the conservative elite to deal with the masses through a mix of cooptation and repression. The factional networks based around family and region established in this period survived into post-independence Philippines (McCoy 2009a, 2009b). The result was a political system in which centrifugal pressures predominated and in which provincial brokers were the linchpins of the network (Hutchcroft 1991). As I describe in Section 5, populist mobilizers could thrive in this system.

Spanish rule in the Philippines took on a different form both to other Western possessions in the region and to Spain's own major colonies in the Americas. The Philippines, or rather Manilla, was incorporated into the colonial economy via the trilateral Galleon trade, which linked Spain to Asian spice and luxury good exchanges through its precious metal mines in Mexico. The Spanish sought to implement the *encomienda* system, in which natives would be coercively organized into working estates under the purview of an *encomendero*, themselves usually military conquerors or their clients. More formal administration followed and as cash crops, especially sugar, expanded, a small number of oligarchs consolidated enormous landed estates and established effective control over the economy.

Toward the end of the nineteenth century, a small cohort of educated elites known as *illustrados*, mostly the sons of the wealthy landed oligarchs, had begun to emerge, and, in 1898, launched a war for independence from Spain. However, American intervention put elites' dreams of immediate independence to an end. Probably motivated more by a desire to prevent rival powers from gaining control over the archipelago than to exploit it for its own purposes, America's early state-building efforts were marked by collaboration with the local elite rather than the building of autonomous state institutions (Abinales 2003). Uniquely among Asian colonial powers, the United States prioritized electoral institutions over bureaucratic ones (Hutchcroft and Rocamora 2003). In part, of course, this was a repetition of American political development, where party building preceded state building (Shefter 1994). The American Governor of the Philippines, William Howard Taft, famously adopted a "policy of attraction" to incorporate and rule through the native landholding elite (Karnow 1990: 173). *Illustrados* flocked to the collaborationist banner under de Partido de Tavera's *Partido Federal* (Cullinane 1989). The *Partido Federal* quickly built up a network of nearly 300 local committees and over 150,000 members (Brands 1992: 66). This, however, did not mean the development of a bureaucratic party system. Rather, by giving the *Federalistas* a monopoly on Filipino government jobs, Taft hoped that de Tavera's party would be able to deploy patronage to concentrate the "conservative forces in the islands" (Karnow 1990: 176). However, the *illustrado* elite were no passive recipients of American patronage. They played the game as brokers extremely well, entrenching themselves as vital intermediaries in the American empire (Constantino and Constantino 1975: 314).

The period in and around independence created a set of political institutions that encouraged the formation of neo-patrimonial networks with little programmatic coherence (Hutchcroft and Rocamora 2003: 266, McCoy 1981: 51). Politicians used the spoils of office not just to enrich themselves, but to build up a base of support autonomous from the national party system (Constantino and Constantino 1975: 319, Sidel 1997: 951). This process only accelerated as the Philippine elite gained access to higher and higher levels of office. Calimbahin (2009: 44–45) quotes George Malcom, an American colonial administrator, as saying "pork barrel has become a necessary evil. 'Pork' is magnanimously allocated in slices in the annual Public Works Act. It matters not that this division of the spoils politics is wasteful and a fecund source of graft."

The general economic depression and growing inequalities of the interwar period, followed quickly by the depredations of Japanese occupation during the Second World War, severely damaged this provincialized patronage-based political system especially in rural Central Luzon. By the late 1930s, agrarian protests had become frequent. Peasants burnt or stole crops, refused to harvest the landlords' share, held parades and marches and so on. Violent uprisings emerged across the province (Kerkvliet 1977). This partial breakdown of patronage relations presented the Philippines' first quasi-populist leader with a political opening. Styling himself as a champion of the people, Manuel Quezon repressed the radicals while attempting to coopt the moderates. For Quezon, even under the constraints on the franchise in operation at the time, appealing directly to the people was a means by which the powerful provincial brokers might be tamed (McCoy 1989: 139–140). Quezon achieved a measure of success in centralizing control over the provincial elite but his efforts would not endure, as I discuss further below.

Indonesia's early political development proceeded somewhat differently. Unlike the Spanish, the Dutch largely adopted a system of indirect rule, meaning that while they imposed industrial and trading monopolies and controlled the foreign affairs of the colony, they left many aspects of administration in the hands of native rulers. The Dutch wrested control of the East Indies from the Portuguese in the seventeenth century and focused their energies on monopolizing the spice trade centered on Maluku. However, competition from the British in particular led the Dutch to develop the colonial economy more intensively. On the island of Java, the Dutch established a more pervasive administrative and economic governing structure. Rather than creating a class of native elite landowners, the Dutch exploited local land and labor through plantations themselves. They introduced a compulsory cash-crop cultivation system, with native farmers being forced to produce set amounts of sugar, coffee, and other crops. Large-scale plantations of tea, cinchona, and rubber were also introduced in the late nineteenth century and the exploitation of minerals such as tin and oil followed. Profits from processing, shipping, and related financial services went to the Netherlands. No class of native oligarchic landlords with interests autonomous from the colonial state comparable to those in the Philippines had emerged by independence (Crouch 1985: 14–15).

Politically, in turn, unlike the Americans in the Philippines, the Dutch sought to suppress, rather than exploit the political aspirations of native Indonesians. A People's Council (*Volksraad*) was set up in 1918, but unlike the Philippines elite who became the nodes in an emerging patron–client network, the Indonesian elite was politically excluded. They in turn were not in a position to incorporate the masses on the same clientelistic terms as occurred in the Philippines and India among other countries in colonial Asia. Traditional rulers in Indonesia were instead made into regents and the aristocratic (though not necessarily wealthy) elite was incorporated into the bureaucratic structure of the Dutch regime of residents and district officers (Vickers 2005: 14). Although native representation on the Council expanded in the late 1920s, it never had much real power.

Economic development, pushed forward by the dominant Liberal Party in the Netherlands, focused on plantation production. Yet the labor regime was harsh and despite economic growth, conditions for most Indonesians failed to improve. Although there was much formal modernization of land law, in practice, peasants were often compelled to perform labor services for the landed elite on plantations of sugar and other crops (Vickers 2005: 38). Indeed, the conversion of common land into individual holdings was exploited by village headmen, leading to increased inequality (Vickers 2005: 45). The mobilization that did subsequently occur thus came from below, with protests, sabotage, and strikes pocking the early decades of the twentieth century. The first sustained wave of proto-nationalist mobilization in the form of the *Sarekat Islam* (SI) was repressed by the Dutch.

After the First World War, the main front of the nationalist movement took on a distinctly socialist character. The Communist Party of Indonesia (PKI) was formally created in 1924 (although it existed under different names previously), and quickly grew in numbers (McVey 1965). Locked out of political participation, the PKI was frequently involved in strike action and demonstrations in the interwar period, but was repressed following a series of abortive uprisings in 1926–1927. With the collapse in demand from the Great Depression taking hold in the late 1920s, unemployment surged and living conditions plummeted. Tens of thousands of Javanese workers sold themselves into indenture to escape starvation. No party, including the PKI, which had by then been heavily supressed, was able to successfully mobilize Indonesians' economic and cultural anxieties. The SI remained the largest political organization in the colony but it never took the form of a mass-based modern political party. The growth of Sukarno's secular party, the National Party (PNI), as an alternative, was inhibited by the Dutch. In repressing rather than coopting elite political forces as clientelistic machines, Dutch policy more closely resembled that of the French in Indochina than the English in India or the Americans in the Philippines.

The Pacific War was marked by both rupture and continuity in Indonesia's political economic order. Dutch resistance to the Japanese crumbled almost instantly after the invasion in 1942. If there was any native enthusiasm for the Japanese overthrow of Dutch rule this was quickly tempered by the brutal occupation and the system of impressment the Japanese employed. The Dutch reoccupied Indonesia after 1945 but any semblance of central authority was gone. Guerrilla resistance to Dutch rule roiled the countryside for the next four years. Tens of thousands of Indonesians were killed and millions were displaced. The economy collapsed, threatening the population with starvation. For the masses, revolt was driven not just by opposition to the Dutch, but to the aristocratic elite that had collaborated with them. Traditional rulers and landowners were attacked in many regions but any hopes of a social revolution were short-lived as most attempts at the armed redistribution of property were crushed.

Like much of Southeast Asia, Thailand's politics were deeply affected by Western imperialism, the disruption of the Pacific War, and the proxy conflicts of the Cold War that played out in the region. Thailand, unlike all of the other major states in Southeast Asia, was never under formal colonial rule, whether of a Western or Eastern power. However, Thailand was incorporated into the world economy in the nineteenth century on much the same terms as neighboring formal colonies. Thailand was a source of rice and later other primary products. However, for the most part, and very much unlike the Philippines, a smallholding rather than landlord-based rural structure prevailed. As of 1937, about three quarters of the land was in the hands of smallholders and production remained geared toward self-sufficiency (Baker and Phongpaichit 2014: 83). Administratively, an aristocratic-bureaucratic elite ruled over this relatively autonomous rice-producing peasantry right through the "revolutionary" period of the 1930s and beyond (Crouch 1985: 16). Agrarian production, although connected to international markets, was not heavily commercialized and the system of rural credit was underdeveloped (Baker and Phongpaichit 2014: 88).

Industrialization was still almost non-existent by the turn of the early twentieth century and urbanization remained very low. Government reluctance to allow the same kind of development of minerals or plantation agriculture (e. g., rubber) as prevailed elsewhere in Southeast Asia put a ceiling on the inflow of Western capital. However, domestic, or at least Chinese-Thai, investment in industries such as rice milling and saw milling began to grow by the First World War. On the back of the development of this primary export industry, some domestic manufacturing of consumer products occurred in the 1920s and 1930s (Baker and Phongpaichit 2014: 92–93). Although rice exports declined from 70 percent of all exports in 1910 to 50 percent by around 1950, the sector still exerted an outsize influence. In the 1930s, just five families dominated the rice milling and export trade. The "rice barons" expanded into finance and related services, building up significant political and economic influence.

Although the Thai monarchy was by no means an effective absolutism, party development nevertheless remained weak. Pridi's People's Party was formed by the Jacobin group of elites and officers who led the 1932 revolution. The party ruled Thailand through the 1930s, but even though it had programmatic ambitions, it lacked connection to a mass base. Indeed, the ruling party remained so concerned about its lack of support vis-à-vis the royalists that it prohibited the formation of competing parties (Baker and Phongpaichit 2014: 122). Gradually, indeed, the military wing of the People's Party began to assume control with the ambition to emulate the militarized Fascist models of Germany and Japan. As the Second World War approached, the government began setting up companies in strategic industries such as oil supply and textiles (Baker and Phongpaichit 2014: 129). The industrialization that did occur was state controlled or subject to heavy regulation. It nevertheless provided the beginnings of an urban working class that could be mobilized in the wake of the disruption of the War and the shortages that it produced. The United Workers of Thailand was set up in 1947 and its membership grew to 60,000 within two years. Mass politics, however, never materialized. Justified by the threat of Communist revolution, the military took power in a coup in 1947. Anti-communist repression, supported if not advocated by the government's American patrons, defined the next two decades. Along with United States military involvement in the region came development aid for its clients. Additionally, a relatively small number of politically well-connected families were able to profit from the establishment of joint manufacturing ventures with foreign, often Japanese, firms (Baker and Phongpaichit 2014: 152).

Although patrimonialism was by no means new to the Philippines, Indonesia, and Thailand, the direct manipulation of political structures by Western imperial powers in the nineteenth and twentieth centuries, and the indirect effects on the social structures of these territories due to their incorporation into the world economy on subordinate terms, had profound implications for political organization in the second half of the twentieth century. First, the possibility of mass-based democratic bureaucratic party organization was curtailed by the lack of nationwide economic modernization, industrialization, and urbanization. Second, where clientelistic incorporation was facilitated, as in the Philippines, political organization was based on the local patronage networks of political elites, with significant latent potential for fragmentation. Where clientelistic incorporation was repressed, as in Indonesia and Thailand, democracy itself would prove even more difficult to sustain. Unlike the Philippines or India, they lacked a national coalition of elite party brokers tied together by the central distribution of rents, who would had sufficient incentives to maintain clientelistic (democratic) party-based rule (Kenny 2017: 63–80).

Establishing (Patronage) Democracy in Southeast Asia

The political and economic legacies of colonialism had a significant impact on party building in Southeast Asia in the latter part of the twentieth century. However, subsequent socioeconomic change, institutional innovation, and external shocks, whether political (e.g., military) or economic, also impacted on party development in the region. This subsection examines the development of party systems in the wake of colonial rule, the assertion of authoritarian control between the 1950s and 1970s, and the (re)establishment of democracy in the latter part of the twentieth century in the Philippines, Indonesia, and Thailand.

The Philippines case illustrates well how careful we have to be about drawing a direct relationship between colonial legacies and post-colonial outcomes. The patronage system that had become increasingly centralized in the late 1930s came apart with remarkable speed as a consequence of the Pacific War. In the Philippines, the Japanese occupation during the War had the effect of drastically weakening the central state apparatus. As central patronage was cut off, provincial brokers grabbed the resources of the state, establishing de facto control over the implementing powers of the government. In the chaos, the licit economy collapsed. Steinberg (1967: 90) writes that the "black market became the only market." Many strongmen, including Ferdinand Marcos, took advantage, smuggling and profiting from the new illicit trade. After the war, these so-called "warlords" were not easily shifted (McCoy 2009b: 14). Instead, the weakness of the state compelled the national leadership into major concessions with the provincial brokers both from the old oligarchy and the new bosses. Successive Filipino presidents would struggle to reestablish the degree of control over the patronage network that Quezon had achieved in the 1930s.

Despite their personally authoritarian tendencies, the dominant elites at the time of independence were well served by a nationally democratic system with weak enforcement capabilities. Elites remained fearful of the military and chose to keep it divided and weak. Democracy, though imperfect, had proven an acceptable medium for channeling intra-elite competition for dominance. Thus, while democracy was restored after independence, it was now unrestrained by American supervision or internal checks and balances on the prerogatives of the political elite. After the war, "local Filipino elites and the national oligarchy were able to extract concessions from the executive that breached the insulation of the regulatory bureaucracy, removing any restraint on pure rent seeking" (McCoy 2009a: xv). Because of the need to maintain a two-thirds majority in the Senate, the administration was utterly dependent on elite support from below. This put the oligarchy and the bosses in a commanding negotiating position. McCoy (2009b: 7) writes:

> After independence in 1946, moreover, the Philippine central government effectively lost control over the countryside to regional politicians, some so powerful that they became known as warlords. Reinforcing their economic power and political offices with private armies, these warlords terrorized the peasantry and extracted a de facto regional autonomy as the price for delivering their vote banks to Manila politicians.

The result was to be a highly fragmented political system that was prone to populist and authoritarian reaction. Through to Marcos's declaration of martial law in 1972, the Philippines retained a two-party system, but these parties were far from bureaucratic. The Liberals and the Nacionalistas traded power, but political competition was between patronage networks not coherent societal interest groups. Internally, the major parties continued to be weak and whichever candidate won the presidency then won over this fractious elite through the distribution of patronage. With the post-war expansion of the franchise, initially, the old methods of mobilizing voters through patronage distribution continued as in the pre-war period. Hutchcroft and Rocamora (2003: 271) write that, "At first, patron–client ties and deeply embedded traditions of social deference were sufficient. The organizational requirements of electoral campaigning remained relatively simple, as elites built factional coalitions in ascending order of complexity from the municipal level upward to the provincial and national levels."

However, the campaign of Ramon Magsaysay in 1953 marked a partial departure from this clientelistic mode of mobilization. Party identification remained almost non-existent. So free were party loyalties that both parties – Liberals and Nacionalistas – had attempted to nominate Magsaysay as their candidate before he ultimately defected from the Liberals to join with the Nacionalistas (Cullather 1993: 321). The critical innovation of Maygsaysay was to supplement "the traditional reliance on patron–client ties with direct campaign appeals to the people" (Hutchcroft and Rocamora 2003: 273). Magsaysay campaigned across the country, seeking to establish direct personal contact with Filipino peasants (Kerkvliet 1977: 238). As one academic commentator noted during the 1953 presidential campaign, Magsaysay's main strength came "not from a personal political machine, but rather from a groundswell of popular revolt against professional politicians" (Hart 1953: 67). His campaign used slogans like "Magsaysay is My Guy" seeking to make the campaign about Magsaysay's personal character rather than about party (Cullather 1993: 305). Rural voters played a central role in Magsaysay's victory as he sought to bypass the traditional electoral machines (Starner 1961). Magsaysay of course still cut deals with local strongmen, powerful businesses, and even the church (Cullather 1993). However, the degree of elite logrolling that occurred was in large part due to Magsaysay's personal popularity among voters. Magsaysay, in other words, leveraged his support among the populace against the political elite. Although the word populist isn't typically used to describe Magsaysay, his mobilization of the masses marked a new organizational form in Philippines politics. Hutchcroft and Rocamora (2003: 273) write:

> the expansion of radio and television in the 1960s, amplified the impact of
> changes brought about by Magsaysay's direct appeals and the rise of more

complex political machines. National campaigns now had to be organized on the basis of the segmentation of the vote into what can be called the "controlled vote" mobilized by local party leaders and that portion of the vote freer of such control and requiring increasingly elaborate media-oriented campaigns.

This movement toward the direct top-down mobilization of voters persisted long after Magsaysay and indeed intensified in the ensuing years. Ferdinand Marcos relied in part on a combination of well-established carrots and sticks to gain the presidency in 1965. He bought votes and strong-armed locally powerful political and business elites into supporting his campaign. Yet, as with Magsaysay before him, Marcos also sought to link directly with voters in the Philippine countryside. In collaboration with his American political consultants, Marcos executed a sophisticated media campaign. Radio remained the primary means of connecting with the masses but film images were also used, with his campaign team loading up projectors and screens and driving them to villages around the country (Johnson 2016: 126).

The political fragmentation that had dogged the early independence government persisted through the authoritarian period of the 1970s and 1980s. Even though Marcos clipped the wings of some oligarchs during the period of martial law (1972–1981), as a group, the oligarchs retained the key roles as intermediaries between the central government and citizens below. Marcos's regime, in spite of its repressive tendencies, did not fundamentally alter the nature of political power in the Philippines (Hutchcroft 2011). In part this was because the elite did not face strong incentives to strengthen the central Philippine state, as say, elites in Malaysia and Singapore did (Slater 2010). By the 1970s, the Communist threat to the elite had essentially been nullified. The peasantry remained trapped in oligarch-dominated patronage networks. Economic developments during the period did little to help. Although during Marcos's period of rule the adoption of "green technologies" in the agricultural sector approximately doubled rice yields, agrarian inequality remained extraordinarily high and the rural oligarchy deeply entrenched.[7] In fact, the main beneficiaries of the green revolution in the Philippines ended up being the elite, who had access to the capital and resources necessary to gain access to government subsidies and take advantage of the scientifically engineered crops.

Likewise, the return to democracy in 1986 did little to fundamentally strengthen political parties in the Philippines. Hutchcroft (1998) characterized the post-Marcos Philippines as an elitist democracy that supported "booty

---

[7] Rachel A. G. Reyes, "Marcos' green revolution," *The Manila Times*, 22 February 2016, www.manilatimes.net/marcos-green-revolution/246377/, accessed 23 August 2018.

capitalism." Provincial elites continue to be the linchpins in the country's political system. Their power is indicated by the extraordinary extent of discretionary funding (i.e., pork) to which each Philippine senator and congressman is entitled. Parties remain very weak. It is not unusual for legislators to switch parties multiple times in a single period of government. Legislative coalitions in the Philippines are formed on the basis of favor trading and the discretionary distribution of government funds. Clans are the "real parties," according to Simbulan (2007: 33). Clans rule the national legislature, too. Co et al. (2005) found that for the 12th Congress (2001–2004), half of the representatives came from established families. Patron–client ties are vital to Philippine clan politics where clients are tied to patrons through debts of honor (*utang na loob*), godparenthood, and other means. In short, in spite of some economic modernization, the basis of political control did not significantly change during Marcos's tenure.

In the Philippines, as Marcos's authority weakened in the mid-1980s, populist mobilization became a potent and recurring electoral strategy (Thompson 2010). Cory Aquino, the widow of assassinated opposition leader Benigno "Ninoy" Aquino, became the figurehead of a mass movement to oust Marco and restore democracy. Cory's leadership of the pro-democracy movement had some clearly charismatic qualities as the movement was loosely organized and heavily associated with her personally. In power, however, Cory soon normalized, becoming entrenched in the clientelistic and clan-based politics of the country.

Cory, like her predecessors, was unable to build a cohesive patronage-based party machine due to the entrenched power of the country's major political families. Parties in the Philippines thus continue to have extremely shallow roots. Survey data going back almost twenty years shows that Filipinos simply do not feel close to their political parties (Figure 2). Never less than 80 percent and sometimes as many as 97 percent of survey respondents do not report feeling close to a party. Fragmented coalition building through the distribution of patronage and direct populist mobilization competed as modes of political incorporation through the 1990s and 2000s. As Tan (2012: 84) summarizes:

> Usually, the root of a party is first, personality and second, clan/provincial power bases. Provincial power holders draw heavily on patron–client relations to perpetuate their stranglehold over politics. Candidates fund their own campaigns and act as free agents in the legislature, switching parties with ease to advance their individual ambitions. It is common after elections for Filipinos to observe a mad rush out of losing groups and toward the party of a newly elected president. Widespread party

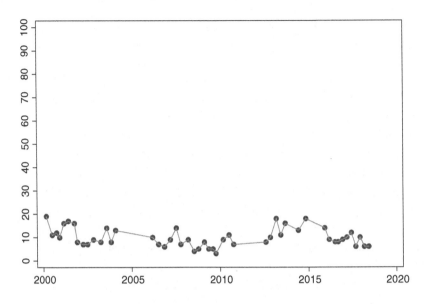

Figure 2 Party Identification (feel close to any party) in the Philippines, Percentage of Filipino Voters
Source: Pulse Asia Surveys

switching contributes to a perception that parties are weak and insubstantial. The Philippine political landscape is peopled by television presenters, singers, and sports greats parlaying their charisma and star power into political office.

Party development followed a different trajectory in Indonesia, but in this case also, by the mid-2000s the party system was characterized by competing clientelistic and populist political organizations. In Indonesia, the Dutch had left behind almost no legacy of industrialization; indeed, if anything, colonial rule de-industrialized the archipelago. The concentration on export-oriented agriculture and the relative lack of government welfare left a legacy of high land inequality (Booth 2016: 27–28). Although Indonesia did not have the same elite landlord structure or the same degree of inequality as the Philippines, it remained the case that about a third of peasants owned no land at all. Indonesians were primed for incorporation as the clients of rural big men (if not oligarchs) who could exploit their local position to mediate between government and the people or indeed, to become government agents themselves. The PKI retained its base as a mass party, but by the time that democracy was curtailed in the late 1950s, it was only able to incorporate about a quarter of the populace, falling short of the majority it needed to install a more bureaucratic form of party rule of the left.

The armed resistance to the Dutch reoccupation of Indonesia also tended to inhibit the development of modern bureaucratic political organizations. Leaders of the resistance were divided on whether Indonesia should be democratic at all. Sukarno wanted to impose a one-party state while Syahrir felt that any revolution had to be as much democratic as it was nationalist. Syahrir's views prevailed in the short term, but the result was democracy with weak and personalistic parties. Vickers (2005: 106–07) writes: "The resulting political parties established in the Republic were based on the existing nationalist leadership, that is, leaders or potential leaders established political parties as a vehicle to power, and formed or linked up with militias or factions of the army."

Indonesia's 1950 Constitution created a parliamentary democracy in which, after the 1955 elections, there would be four main competing forces, of which the Communist party (the PKI) was one. The others were: nationalist (the Indonesian National Party or PNI), modernist Muslims (Masjumi), and traditionalist Muslims (Nahdlatul Ulama or NU). The leading figures of these parties were often landlords with substantial clienteles (Aspinall and Berenschot forthcoming). With no single dominant player, such as the LDP in Japan or to a lesser extent the Indian National Congress party, patronage networks remained deeply fragmented with the key nodes devolved to the local level (Mietzner 2014b).

As the preeminent hero of the independence struggle, Sukarno styled himself as a nationalist and populist leader who could represent these competing local and organized factions with a fair hand. In spite of Sukarno's charisma, his party, the PNI, won only a plurality but not a majority of votes in the 1955 election (Willner 1984). Sukarno could neither fully incorporate the PKI nor establish a sufficiently dominant patronage-based network of his own. The result of the 1955 election was a fragmented parliament and a stalemated constitutional assembly that was prorogued when President Sukarno adopted the concept of "guided democracy" from 1957. Sukarno became stridently anti-party, expressed most clearly in a 1956 speech called "Let Us Bury the Parties" (Feith and Castles 1970: 81–83; cited in Tan 2012: 83). All parties were incorporated into the system in a kind of enforced consensus. Sukarno ultimately dissolved the parliament in 1959 and restored the 1945 Constitution (Feith 2007 [1962]), effectively dispensing with the pretense of democracy (Mujani, Liddle et al. 2018: 1).

In 1965, Sukarno himself was removed by a military takeover. His rule had depended on the consent of the PKI and Sukarno kept the peace by distributing a share of the spoils to the party and its supporters. A leftist coup attempt in 1965 was repelled by the military led by Suharto, and the PKI membership was massacred. Under coercion, Sukarno transferred progressively more power to the military until, in 1967, General Suharto himself was named president. Suharto's New Order regime was based on a combination of coercion and cooptation. The organized political left was violently repressed. Other political forces were then coopted into a system of bureaucratic-military rule, the major instrument of which was the Golkar party. While local bosses had obtained control over state patronage under the weak state and party infrastructure inherited by Sukarno in the first decade after independence, under the militarized Suharto regime, it became much more centralized and Java-centric.

Suharto was able to build local bases of support through the Presidential Instruction Programs (*Instruksi Presiden*, or "*Inpres*"), which allowed him to channel grants to local areas to hire workers and build infrastructure. Most provinces depended on central grants for around 80 percent of their revenues. Central control over the distribution of patronage was thus tightly managed (Booth 2014: 35, MacIntyre 1991). In many cases, Javanese were appointed to key political and military positions, which also limited the autonomy of sub-national units. District heads, mayors, and governors were appointed by the central government, while all village heads became direct employees of the central government allowing for further central control (Mietzner 2014b: 51). Suharto also banned parties at the village level, ensuring central administrative dominance over local politics (Carnegie 2008).

As in the Philippines, resistance to authoritarian rule in Indonesia took on some populist characteristics in the form of the then Indonesian Democratic Party (PDI), one of the main organs of the opposition movement during the latter New Order regime. Megawati, the daughter of Sukarno, became the de facto leader of the PDI in 1993 but the government's attempt to remove her split the party into pro- and anti-Megawati camps. The popularity of Megawati's faction, ultimately renamed the PDI-P (Indonesian Democratic Party of Struggle), drew heavily on her personal qualities and reputation. After Suharto fell in 1998, Megawati is probably best characterized as a populist. However, this period didn't last long. PDI-P became the largest party in Indonesia following the first post-Suharto elections in 1999, and Megawati was chosen as Vice-President. Although she solidified her dominance over the PDI-P, as one of the parties of government the party itself very quickly developed a quintessentially clientelistic profile, building its support through the distribution of patronage, especially once Megawati became president in 2001 after Abdurrahman Wahid stepped down.

The transition to democracy during the *Reformasi* period did not, however, see the PDI-P or other new political parties assume control over a single centralized patronage machine. Rather, Indonesia was compelled to embrace regional autonomy in the late 1990s in order to pre-empt separatist pressures (Aspinall 2013a). Beginning in 1999, new laws transferred extensive powers over policy design, service delivery, and budgeting, along with limited taxation powers, to local governments. The devolution of broad powers over local budgets and public sector personnel management transferred enormous patronage powers into the hands of local executive government. Most importantly, local governments were guaranteed a share of the national budget, which would be transferred automatically every year to subnational governments in block grants, thus reducing the power of the center to discipline subnational units by withholding funding. The local executive thus became the key locus in the distribution of patronage giving the brokers who control these positions enormous influence.

Of course, policy-makers and party leaders in Jakarta were wary of the disintegrative pressures that decentralization implied. Onerous registration criteria were introduced that dictated that parties demonstrate to the General Elections Commission that they maintain a nationwide network of branches; these parties are in turn the only ones allowed to field candidates for parliament and to nominate candidates for regional executive head elections. Independents could not run for national elections and presidential candidates had to be nominated by parties. However, even though provincial and ethnonationalist competition has been largely staved off by this institutional engineering, it has not in practice assured a cohesive national party system. National party elites had been hopeful that the method of choosing local executive heads in the early years of decentralization would preserve their influence in the regions. Initially, executive heads of government – provincial governors, city mayors, and *bupati* in rural districts – were appointed by local parliaments that were themselves elected freely for the first time in 1999. They were thus intended to be subject to some party discipline. Yet in practice the contests were riddled with vote-buying in local legislatures when assembly members assembled to negotiate the appointment of the new local leaders. As Michael Buehler observes, "the majority of parliamentarians voted for whoever offered them the most money, leading to the election of local government heads with no or weak ties to parties or to the assemblies dominated by those parties" (Buehler 2010: 270). This process thus ultimately weakened the control of central party leaderships over the appointment process. Direct elections for executive government positions were introduced in 2004, but this process only further weakened the links between national parties and the local executive. With aspirants for office requiring the nomination of local party branches, it became common – in a process known as *sewa perahu* (boat rental) – for branches to "auction" their nomination to wealthy figures who "see the party as providing just a nomination – a ticket to run on – and nothing else" (Qodari 2010: 132). Direct elections thus reoriented clientelist relationships *downwards* toward the local level, and, in the context of the weak mobilizational power of local party branches, created the "need to establish *personal* political machines to mobilize and structure the masses" (Buehler 2014: 170). The consolidation of these personalized patronage systems around individual local leaders, operating with autonomy from the center, was the subject of regular complaint by national bureaucrats and politicians who could no longer control local governments. With the central government having limited success in clawing back administrative and budgetary authority from subnational governments, Indonesia's political parties amended internal regulations to give more authority to central boards to vet candidates for executive positions in the regions in the hopes of promoting the nomination of their own party cadre – considered more dependable – in direct elections. However, in practice, if influential local political brokers fall out with local party branches or the national party leadership, they are able to switch parties easily with the personal networks underpinning their reelection largely intact and ready for reactivation.

As Figure 3 illustrates, party membership has never been high in Indonesia and has fallen steadily since the first measurements in 2004 (Muhtadi 2018: 18). Party identification (individuals who report feeling close to any party) has fallen even more precipitously (Mujani, Liddle et al. 2018: 188).

The 2009 adoption of an open-list form of proportional representation for national and regional assemblies further weakened the national parties and granted yet more autonomy to local politicians (Aspinall 2014a). The result of a Supreme Court decision, this reform was largely independent of the preferences of the national political parties. This new system encouraged candidates to maximize their personal votes, with the result that district-level parliaments have become a site of competition between "a plethora of small clientelistic parties with no roots in society beyond the immediate networks of individual candidates," with concomitantly high levels of volatility in the compositions of local party systems and a hollowing out of local branch organizations (Tomsa 2014: 259). The local branches of party machines decayed and were replaced by multiple small competitors led primarily by local notables with local goals. At the margins, this competition for the spoils of state patronage resulted in an increase in already remarkably high levels of party-system fragmentation (Aspinall 2005). Further changes to registration and threshold requirements saw a swing back toward the incorporation of these local networks within a

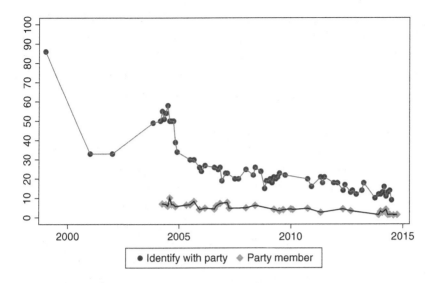

Figure 3 Party Membership (active or inactive) and Party
Identification (feeling close to a party) in Indonesia, Percentage of
Indonesian Voters, 1999–2014
Source for party membership: Muhtadi (2018: 18)
Source for party ID: Mujani, Liddle et al. (2018: 188)

smaller number of larger parties in 2014. It remains the case, however, that national party control over these subnational broker-client networks is relatively weak, whether they are formally inside or outside the parties.

The decentralization of patronage in Indonesia, and its decoupling from ostensibly centralized party organizations, has had knock-on effects for political competition at the national level. The patronage networks built to support the winning and maintenance of power at the subnational level are not effective tools in a presidential campaign; Indonesian candidates for presidential office seem to be increasingly skeptical of their relevance. Essentially autonomous subnational brokers are unreliable partners for national party leaders. For their part, local brokers have little to gain from investing time and money in higher-order election campaigns (Aspinall 2005). Loyalty problems are severe in Indonesia because the links between parties and brokers are so tenuous (Aspinall and Berenschot forthcoming).

The economic development of the country since the New Order has done little to suggest that these trends will change any time soon, indicating the powerful effect of path dependency on party system change. Although a private "capitalist" elite has developed in post-authoritarian Indonesia, it remains embedded in sectors such as resource extraction, finance, telecoms, and construction, where particularistic access to licenses and government contracts facilitates rather than challenges prevailing patterns of rent-seeking and corruption (Aspinall 2013b). Moreover for those among the business class who are ethnic Chinese, any challenge to the political status quo represents a considerable risk.

As most other states in the region experimented with democracy in the wake of the Second World War, Thailand doubled down on authoritarianism. The group of leaders who had dominated Thai politics through the 1930s consolidated their control of the economy through positions in banking, trading, and other sectors. Although the 1950s was characterized by the expansion of agribusiness and import-substituting industrialization, political incorporation into bureaucratic parties was stifled by the persistence of authoritarian rule. In Indonesia, the PKI experienced a sustained period in which it could operate above ground, even successfully contesting the 1955 parliamentary elections; in contrast, the Communist party in Thailand was always smaller and was more consistently and easily suppressed. The same class of indentured and landless laborers on which other Communist parties in the region built did not exist (Crouch 1985: 34, 38–39). Even after the end of hostilities in 1945, the Communist Party of Thailand (CPT) did not attempt to mobilize the peasantry into a mass movement, but remained more an urban organization. Before the party could begin to translate its influence in the labor movement into political capital, another coup in 1947 suspended its progress. The Communist Central Labor Union was outlawed and its leaders arrested. Thailand's further turn to the anti-communist camp in the 1950s and 1960s under a succession of military regimes meant the continued suppression of political organization on the left. The CPT engaged in scattered armed resistance in the late 1960s and early 1970s, but by the time democracy arrived, the party was essentially defunct. Less spectacular, but perhaps of more consequence, was the Peasants Federation of Thailand (PFT), which was concentrated in the area around Chiang Mai. The PFT mobilized thousands in its campaign for lower rents and an effort to fight corruption. Student protests also gathered pace and in the face of both rural and urban discontent the King withdrew his support of the military regime, appointing a National Convention to draw up a new Constitution under which elections were to be held in 1975. The Democratic Party won a plurality but could not form a majority government (Phongpaichit and Baker 1995: 298–303). Fresh elections in 1976 failed to resolve the deadlock.

The growing radicalism of the student movement and the success of Communist forces in neighboring Vietnam and Cambodia gave renewed impetus to the forces of reaction. Counterinsurgency campaigns intensified and the police stepped up their harassment of leftist parties. The red scare culminated in the massacre of students at Thammasat University in October 1976. The King endorsed the military regime of Thanin Kraivichien and the student movement was repressed. In 1978, a new constitution was promulgated, this one lasting until 1991. The new Assembly allowed for the development of political parties. However, its freedom to exercise real authority was constrained by the military and the monarchy. The Thai parties that did develop when democracy tentatively emerged were essentially associations of factions made up of provincial and local powerbrokers and their clients. Thus, long after the introduction of democracy in 1973 and the return of competitive elections in 1979, and still nearly a decade after its further democratic deepening in 1993, formal party organizations still had only a shallow penetration into large parts of the country.

Part of the reason was that in the 1980s, "new provincial business interests, buoyed up by the cash crop economy, learnt how to control the franchise. They invaded the Parliament, captured the political parties, and used parliamentary power for their own ends" (Phongpaichit and Baker 1995: 323). Local notables, whose power derived from their control over agrarian production and the associated local services that built up around it, dominated the National Assembly. The power centers of the three major political parties, the Democrats, Chat Thai, and Social Action, all shifted from Bangkok to the provinces over the course of the 1980s (Phongpaichit and Baker 1995: 340–346). This led to a significant imbalance of political influence of the rural bosses and an apparent development of regional and local political parties. However, as Hicken (2006b) notes, to the extent that there is an association between Thai parties and particular regions, this association has nothing to do with policy differences, but is largely due to the local orientation of the patronage-based factional ties between supporters and individual politicians or political factions, known as *phuak*. Hicken (2006a: 389) writes:

> politicians, and the political parties they created, tended to respond to narrow rather than national constituencies. Parties were focused on the interests of a relatively narrow group of supporters and hence directed the resources of government – often in the form of pork, patronage, rents, etc. – toward that end. Programmatic political parties that appealed to broad national constituencies via national public goods/ policies were largely absent from the political system.

Thus, as In Indonesia and the Philippines, the Thai party system is inexplicable without understanding the role of patronage-based mobilization by provincial brokers. Numerous studies have documented the predominant role that vote buying plays in Thai elections (Arghiros 2001, Callahan and McCargo 1996, Hicken 2002). Forty-five parties took part in the 1975 elections and twenty-one won seats. Parties were the "personal followings of individual leaders, or fronts for the autocratic cliques who control political power" (Prizzia 1985: 88). In the exemplary case of Supharnburi province, documented in detail by Nishizaki (2011), the intermediary role of provincial political elites such as Barnharn allowed them to claim personal credit for state development initiatives, in the process building up a substantial personal following. This pattern is repeated all across rural Thailand. Petty local notables utilize their access to government to buy voters and in turn to amass substantial private fortunes for themselves. Robertson (1996) calls these individuals "rural network politicians."

Parties are in turn beholden to these provincial bosses, who exploit control over material resources to gain political power and vice versa. McCargo (1997) has argued that authentically Thai parties are those dominated by money and personality. They function to distribute and allocate resources, and thus primarily exist in order to "marshal funds and appropriate power" (McCargo, 1997: 118). Murray (1996: 36) describes the system succinctly:

> Most parties, particularly those based on patronage, are unencumbered by ideologies, and many politicians merely use a party as a base from which to serve their own interests; some may change parties eight or more times in their political careers. In a sense, parties win or lose elections before a vote is cast, depending on how effective they are in attracting incumbent politicians with established canvassing networks and patronage links.

Even in the 1990s, the prospects for electoral success for Thai politicians depended on factional support rather than any party imprimatur, with the result that factions have more influence over candidate selection and behavior than do parties (Ockey 1994). Research by Chambers (2008) further shows that factions had much greater influence than parties on government stability. McCargo and Patthamānan (2005: 71) write that "Factions were typically organized around key individuals who supplied leadership and financial support; these individuals could readily move their faction from one party to another in search of greater opportunities and benefits, thereby destabilizing political parties, causing them regularly to fragment and then reconstruct." Indeed, the party may not be a very useful framework for understanding Thai politics through the end of the 1990s. McCargo (1997) argues that to even search for a bureaucratic party in Thailand in the pre-Thaksin period is anachronistic.

It is true that the Thai electoral system has traditionally encouraged the formation of personal vote banks rather than party loyalty (Hicken 2002). However, as I argued in Section 2, it may be problematic to assign a causal role to electoral institutions. In this case, a system that encouraged personalization suited the interests of these provincial Thai elites. In any case, even reforms that consolidated the number of parties did little to alter the basic underlying structure of Thai politics. The 1981 Political Party Act proscribed small parties, with the result that local bosses simply became the heads of factions within larger party structures (McCargo 1997: 120).

The lack of bureaucratic party development in Thailand poses an additional question. From the 1960s through to the mid-1990s, Thailand's economic growth was among the most rapid in the world. While more than 80 percent of the population was employed in agriculture in 1960, this figure was just 48 percent in 1997. Manufactured exports grew from just 1 percent of total exports in 1960 to 80 percent by the mid-1990s (Hewison 2000). However, as in the Philippines and Indonesia, urbanization and industrialization, even though further advanced, did not give rise to a bureaucratic party system. A number of factors may explain why.

First, the gains of Thailand's modernization were concentrated overwhelmingly in Bangkok and its environs. Large parts of the Thai peasantry, where limited modernization had occurred, remained incorporated into the political and economic networks of rural leaders (Walker 2012), while urban migrants were incorporated into the clientelistic networks of the cities' parties. The contrast with other fast-developing economies in Northeast Asia such as South Korea is stark (Walker 2015).

Second, the indicators of development used by Hewison (2000) and others overstate the degree of socioeconomic transformation entailed in Thailand's growth. Thailand's growth has been based on increased factor inputs rather than increased productivity (Doner 2009); that is, more on sweat than on ingenuity. Although such growth might be expected to facilitate the development of union-based politics, as say in north-western Europe in the nineteenth century, workers alone have not been able to engineer the development of a bureaucratic party system. Bureaucratic party systems depend as much on the formation of organized conservative and liberal parties as they do labor parties. Thailand's economic transformation gave rise to the development of a small industrial and financial, and even outward looking elite, who might have been expected to support such party system reforms. However, large parts of the economic elite remained clients of the (authoritarian) state (Hutchcroft 1999), deeply entrenched in the political and financial networks of the monarchy. Rather than fostering a robust civil society, the dominance of the state over industrialization thus meant that the process did not aid the formation of class-based parties in the way it had historically done in the West.

This leads to a third related factor. The Thai king is no mere constitutional figurehead. In an influential, although perhaps somewhat dated article, Duncan McCargo (2005) characterized Thai politics in terms of a "network monarchy." He writes: "Network monarchy is a form of semi-monarchical rule: the Thai King and his allies have forged a modern form of monarchy as a para-political institution" (McCargo 2005: 501). The King regularly intervened in politics, including the formation of governing coalitions, through privy councillors and trusted military figures. In times of crisis, decision-making reverted to the monarch alone as the main source of political legitimacy. The King's repeated insertion in the political system meant that parties remained weak, and more-over, highly personalized institutions, in which connections to the network surrounding the monarchy were more important than ties with voters. The result has been that bureaucratic incorporation of voters into political parties in Thailand has remained weak in spite of it being the most developed of the democratic Southeast Asian economies. In the 2000s, as the next section of this Element shows, politics in Thailand became a three-way contest between the local political elite, whose autonomy waxes and wanes over time, a bureau-cratic-military-monarchical network with little commitment to democracy, and a populist movement led by Thaksin Shinawatra that sought to outflank both of the others by appealing directly to the people.

Economies, Institutions, and Fragmented Parties

This section concludes with some general comparative lessons on why parties are so fragmented in Southeast Asia. First, in a proximate sense, the adoption of decentralized and candidate-focused electoral institutions has empowered local elites over centralized party leaderships. Ultimately, however, electoral institu-tions are in large part endogenous to existing power structures; the political and economic power of the subnational elite is one of the reasons why these decentralizing institutions were put in place. In any case, even more centralized formal institutions have typically failed to result in the consolidation of bureau-cratic parties. Institutional engineering to counter these effects has done little to make parties in the region stronger or to prevent populists from coming to power. In Thailand, Indonesia, and even Myanmar the need for party building in order to contest elections is on paper substantial. In theory, this might have created bureaucratic parties, based on deeply rooted civil society organizations, layers of party management, and collective leadership. However, as will become clear in the next section, institutional design alone is insufficient to bring such parties into existence. As both the Indonesian and Thai cases make clear, charismatic leaders have been able to appeal directly to voters, irrespective of the institutional rules enshrined in these countries.

The case of Timor-Leste illustrates well the limits of what institutional design can achieve. Timor-Leste has a population of just 1.2 million and an electorate of about 750,000, making it possible for it to have just a single national district, in which voters do not choose representatives of their own locality, but national representatives. Moreover, they can only choose their preferences for a party, with members of parliament then being determined by their order on closed party lists in proportion to the votes their party receives. These institutional features should mitigate the role of charisma in party–voter linkages. However, after only a single electoral cycle, the power of charisma to drive electoral results was demonstrated with Gusmão becoming Prime Minister under the newly created CNRT in 2007. The lesson is clear: without political economic foundations, institutions by themselves are insufficient to build bureaucratic parties. Indeed, the institutions that work well in one context may be ineffective – or worse – in another (Przeworski 2004).

Second, the political economy of the region's major democracies has fostered weak and fragmented parties. For much of the post-war period, the economies of democratic Southeast Asia remained dependent on agriculture and other primary industries. Both tended to reinforce the position of subnational economic elites who gained their prominence either through their position as landholders or as beneficiaries of government patronage. Although modern export-oriented manufacturing and service industries have developed in democratic Southeast Asia, especially in Thailand, their effects remain geographically concentrated, while business leaders are often deeply imbricated in government-industry networks. Moreover, once fragmented patronage based systems are entrenched, they become extremely difficult to reform. The more widely fragmented patronage-based party systems are, the more veto players there are to resist further centralization and bureaucratization irrespective of subsequent economic development (Kenny 2015b). Patronage-based party systems are thus extremely "sticky" institutions (Shefter 1994).

Third, the institutional and economic legacies of colonial rule and imperial influence have played a major role. While authoritarian rule in South Korea and Taiwan saw the development of strong administrative states and major, modern industrialized sectors of the economy, with the exception of Singapore and to a lesser extent Malaysia, similar dynamics did not emerge under authoritarian rule in Southeast Asia. Agency surely mattered, but it would be erroneous to put all of this down to the enlightenment of the former's dictators and the capriciousness of the latter's. Northeast and Southeast Asia were left with very different physical and human capital inheritances (Booth 1999). South Korea and Taiwan had orders of magnitude more developed infrastructure in terms of railways and electricity at the time of independence. They also had much more developed state infrastructures, namely indigenous bureaucracies, that made possible the programmatic industrializing reforms that these countries undertook in the 1960s, 70s, and 80s. The result, with the consolidation of democracy in the 1990s, was the gradual development of relatively more bureaucratic party systems in South Korea and especially Taiwan.

5 Populist Leaders

The fragmented nature of clientelistic party organizations across democratic Southeast Asia has provided regular opportunities for charismatic political campaigners to come to power by establishing direct linkages with voters. In recent years in particular, this form of political organization, in its full and partial forms, has been pervasive; Duterte, Yudhyono, and Thaksin have all been able to come to power through personal electoral vehicles that made direct appeals to voters who are only weakly attached – if at all – to establishment parties. This section will concentrate on the rise of these three contemporary populists, but will also look to place their success in comparative perspective.

Little-known outside Davao City on the southern island of Mindanao, where he had been mayor since 1988, in late 2016, Rodrigo Duterte came to the presidency of the Philippines as a populist, anti-establishment candidate, promising to scale up the "strongman" rule that he honed in his home city. In power, he has waged a violent campaign against drug-related criminality, with estimates of the number of those killed in the first eighteen months of his presidency running as high as 12,000. This is already many times the number estimated to have been executed under nearly a decade of martial law under Marcos (Thompson 2016a). Experts have suggested that Duterte's regime is an "illiberal democracy," as he has told Filipinos themselves to "forget the laws" in the effort to impose "order" (Thompson 2017). Randy David has termed his brand of "tough guy" rule *Dutertismo*, while the president himself welcomes the nickname "Duterte Harry" after Clint Eastwood's quasi-vigilante character in the Dirty Harry series of movies (Miller 2018).

Why exactly did Duterte appeal to Filipino voters? First, and most important from a theoretical perspective, is the almost total absence of bureaucratic political parties from the equation (see Figure 2). Any Filipino politician is thus likely to rely on some combination of material inducements and charisma. In presidential races, material inducements can take the form of direct payment for votes or a more indirect form in which vote banks are mobilized by regionally dominant brokers. Charismatic appeals delivered through mass rallies and the mass media may draw on a prior record of achievement or on the kinds of cross-cutting issues identified above, such as immigration, nationalism, or corruption, which allow them to mobilize a potentially winning coalition of supporters. Can we say which strategy Duterte relied on? Not conclusively, but we do have some suggestive evidence.

Duterte, perhaps in spite of appearances, is a highly shrewd, calculating politician. He in fact repeatedly refused to announce a run for the presidency as he allowed rivals to concentrate their fire on one another. From early 2015 until he formally threw his hat into the ring by filing as a substitute for a party-mate in late November 2016, Duterte had toured the country promoting a federalist agenda. He thus quietly built up a network of supporters across the country, waiting until some key rivals had dropped in the polls and the calls for him to run reached a sufficient pitch. Although Duterte's political organization is highly personalistic, like other presidential candidates, he seems to have incorporated local broker networks that bought votes in the run up to his 2016 election. How important was this strategy to Duterte? Survey data on the prevalence of vote buying prior to the 2016 election shows that 18.5 percent of voters were offered a material inducement for their vote. Of those, about 80 percent accepted the money or other bribe. However, only 20.4 percent of those accepting bribes claim to have actually voted for the candidate who "bought" their vote. That's equivalent to saying that just 2.8 percent votes were successfully bought. Even then, of course, we might assume that some voters could have chosen the same candidate even in the absence of such an inducement. Among the presidential candidates, Duterte supporters were no more or less likely than those of other candidates to have received a bribe for their vote.[8] Overall, in other words, the effect of outright vote buying on Duterte's support in the election was probably marginal. Comparatively, we know that most effective vote buying tends to be done by local candidates (Aspinall and Berenschot forthcoming).

Duterte instead seems to have relied much more heavily on his charisma to appeal directly to voters. Once launched, his campaign promoted the slogan "change is coming" although it remained unclear what the content of this change would be. Duterte was vaunted as the "man on horseback" who would challenge the establishment, or as he put it, "Imperial Manila." Duterte's abstract promises were complemented by the slogan *tapang at malasakit* (courage and compassion), a characterization first put out in a video circulated on social media in late May 2015. His campaign subsequently used the phrase in its other ads, this time directly linking the traits with Duterte

---

[8] Pulse Asia Research Inc. Survey, July 2016.

through the phrase *Tapang at Malasakit si Duterte* (Duterte is courageous and compassionate). Fusing the first syllable of each trait, the shortened message becomes *Tama si Duterte* (Duterte is right) (Holmes 2016). Beyond these platitudes, Duterte's election "manifesto" was so vague on policy terms that observers have argued that his appeal can only be explained in non-rational terms (Curato 2017). His sister, Eleanor, said, "He is being used as a vehicle of the Holy Spirit" (Miller 2018: 15), while he himself seems to believe that it is his destiny to lead his country. From his campaign through his early presidency, Duterte was known for holding enormous political rallies, which were popular in part because of his attraction as a showman. He has gone to combat zones, urban poor communities, and areas affected by natural disasters, among others, to speak directly with "regular" Filipinos. While his language is often derisive, misogynistic, and vulgar, it is common to hear his audience applaud or laugh at his controversial statements, especially when he ridicules his critics (Casiple 2016).

Duterte also relied heavily on mass media and social media to deliver his message directly to voters. Most Filipino registered voters (77 percent) say that television was the most influential source of information for them in their vote choice for president.[9] The significant increase in pre-election support for Duterte (from 24 percent in March 2016 to 35 percent in April 2016) can be partially attributed to his strong performance in the second presidential debate, which was aired live by major television and radio networks. In an April 2016 survey, a plurality (34 percent) of respondents who watched, listened to, or read reports about the debate believed that Duterte outperformed the other contenders.[10] Beyond the debates, Duterte, given his controversial and often crude behavior, commanded extensive airtime. He also had – and has – an army of online supporters who vigorously defend him on social media, shouting down and even threatening his critics. However, despite the attention that observers have paid to social media in explaining Duterte's support, only 2.7 percent of voters said that this was their main source of information in their vote choice. Even in the Philippines, it seems that television remained paramount as of 2016.

Another indication that Duterte relied on his charismatic appeal comes in the role played by his unusual focus on crime. In the months before the election, Duterte began to aggressively campaign on the issue of drug-related criminality. Duterte drew on his reputation as the strongman mayor of Davao City, vowing to rid the country of illegal drugs within six months of his confirmation.

---

[9] Pulse Asia Research Inc. Survey, March 2016
[10] Pulse Asia Research Inc. Survey, April 2016

In early March 2016, he pronounced that if elected president, he would kill thousands of criminals, the funeral parlours would be packed, and he would dump 100,000 of the slain criminals in Manila Bay where the fish would grow fat. He was known for saying: "If you are not prepared to kill and be killed, you have no business being president of this country."[11] As a policy issue, crime, like corruption, fits well in the populist mobilization strategy; few voters are likely to oppose the idea of reducing crime or corruption, thus allowing the populist to appeal to a broad, even cross-class, constituency of individual voters. Indeed, in the Philippines, surveys indicate that fewer than 5 percent of voters disapprove of Duterte's campaign against illegal drugs (Kenny and Holmes 2018).

The issue of crime is so commonly exploited by populists that it has its own nomenclature. *Penal populism* refers to an understanding of justice in which criminal and anti-social activity should be punished, and punished harshly. It is based on the premise that too often the legal system works to the advantage of criminals and society's already privileged. Penal populism implies that criminal justice should be informed by the views of "ordinary individuals rather than . . . elite opinion" (Pratt 2007: 5). This understanding of justice goes along with a preference for strong leadership. Penal populists are charismatic leaders who rely more on plebiscitary norms of legitimacy than on rules, institutions, and regularized procedures. People who believe that a leader is endowed with charisma should have less of an attachment to laws and procedures per se. In this sense, belief in a leader's charisma should be associated with support for order over law (Kenny and Holmes 2018). Duterte unquestionably drew attention to the issue of drug-related criminality in the lead up to the 2016 election. His willingness to ignore legal procedure and punish crime directly seems to have won over many voters.

Finally, we can draw on some novel data on the degree to which individuals view Duterte as a "charismatic" as opposed to "regular" leader. Kenny and Holmes (2018) asked survey respondents to give an open-ended description of Duterte in a word or sentence. They then employed a crowd-sourced non-expert text analysis of these descriptions in which coders were asked to determine whether the description was of a charismatic or non-charismatic leader (Benoit, Conway et al. 2016).[12] They found that 42 percent of

---

[11] Randy David, "Dutertismo," *Philippine Daily Enquirer*, 1 May 2016, http://opinion.inquirer .net/94530/dutertismo#ixzz554QleIXs

[12] Non-expert coders were instructed as follows: "Each of the following words or sentences was used by respondents in a recent survey to describe some political leaders. We would like you to say whether you think the respondent believes the leader in question to be 'charismatic.' A charismatic leader is one who people believe to be gifted with extraordinary personal qualities. Respondents who believe that a leader is charismatic may describe him or her as heroic,

respondents ascribed charismatic leadership traits to Duterte. As we would anticipate, belief in Duterte's charisma is strongly correlated with trust in Duterte, approval of Duterte's performance, and support for the campaign against illegal drugs (Kenny and Holmes 2018). However, as I noted in Section 2, we lack the dynamic social-psychological data to adequately address the direction of cause and effect between support for Duterte (or other populist candidates) and populist attitudes or belief in a leader's charisma.

What is clear, however, is that support for Duterte was completely unrelated to support for any particular party (including his own). Duterte won the 2016 election in a landslide by appealing to voters independently of a party, portraying himself as the individual leader who alone could address disorder in the Philippines. In this respect, Duterte is an extreme example of an established practice in the Philippines (McCoy 2017). Even in 2016, one of Duterte's competitors, the incumbent Vice President under Aquino, Jejomar Binay, was at least partially populist. As mayor of Makati City for over twenty years, Binay had developed a reputation for personalizing power, reorienting "the machinery of Makati politics around his person as its peerless boss" (Garrido 2013: 179). Binay sought to directly connect with his supporters, from attending funerals to eating with his hands in town feasts (Curato 2017: 144). Binay instituted welfare policies to help the poor and used this to build a reputation as an anti-elite candidate. Corruption allegations dogged Binay's campaign but had he won, we could very easily be analysing him as a prominent Southeast Asian populist.

Not long before Duterte or Binay, one of the most influential leaders in post-Marcos Philippines was Joseph Ejercito Estrada, or "Erap" as he was widely known. Erap relied primarily on his celebrity as an actor to top the presidential polls in 1998. Estrada, like populists before and after him, ran a highly personalistic campaign, yet like Cory Aquino, he relied to a significant degree on supporting coalitions of brokers who supported his campaign. He was thus more of a *partial* populist than Duterte. Hedman (2001) notes two particular campaign messages deployed by Estrada: *JEEP ni Erap*, which literally means "Erap's Jeep." As an acronym, JEEP refers to "Justice, Economy, Environment, and Peace" and simultaneously to "Joseph Ejercito Estrada for President"; the jeep itself continues to be the most common means of public transportation throughout the Philippines. *Erap para sa Mahirap* simply means "Erap for the Poor." Unlike Duterte therefore, Estrada concentrated his policy appeals in narrower class terms, which tended to limit his appeal. Estrada's

---

infallible, or superlative in some other way. This is in contrast to "regular" leaders who people typically describe in terms of professional competences, policies, or achievements. Do these listed words/phrases suggest that the leader being described is charismatic?"

success, like Duterte's, was in part due to the persistent fragmentation of the Philippine party system in the post-Marcos era. There were some eleven contenders for the presidency in 1998 and despite the poor polling numbers that many of them had in comparison with Estrada, they refused to consolidate their opposition behind any one or two viable candidates. Estrada was in fact the one to best exploit the divisions of the Philippine parties in his bid for power. Faced by no dominant opposition party, he assembled a coalition of three parties to support his bid with their political machines in return for the promise of patronage when he had won the presidency (Bolongaita 1999). As the cases of Duterte, Binay, and at least partially, Estrada and Cory Aquino suggest, populism is virtually a Philippines condition (McCoy 2017).

Across the Sulawesi Sea, since the introduction of direct presidential elections in 2004, Indonesia saw a rapid shift toward personalistic and populist campaigns in which presidential candidates' reliance on party machinery and clientelist networks has grown less and less important relative to the pull of charismatic campaigns from the center. As Liddle and Mujani (2007: 839) conclude, voters are "strongly attached to national party leaders, an attachment that appears to be a principal reason for voting for political party or for president." The 2004 election saw a three-way contest between then president Megawati (PDI-P), Wiranto, as Chairman of Golkar, and Yudhoyono, a former army general and cabinet minster, who took over leadership of *Partai Demokrat* (PD). Megawati and the other party chiefs backing her candidacy were confident of victory despite her personal unpopularity, due to the overwhelming organizational advantages held by her party coalition: specifically, following the elimination of Wiranto in the first round of elections, her campaign had the combined support of PDI-P and Golkar, the latter being the second-largest party and the organization with the most residual influence over local political leaders and bureaucrats thanks to its legacy as the political party of the Suharto regime. Yet the election was won by the relative outsider, Yudhoyono.

PD, an essentially new party with a minor presence in national and local parliaments, was a classic populist vehicle lacking meaningful connections, clientelist or otherwise, to a constituency beyond its appeal as the party of a popular national figure (Dagg 2007). The PD was created by opponents of Megawati in 2002, incorporating disenfranchised members of Golkar and a wide range of other political aspirants in an effort to meet the national registration threshold required to contest the presidency. The viability of the party, however, relied heavily on the personal appeal of Yudhoyono, even though his initial commitment to a presidential run under the PD label was lukewarm (Honna 2012). Once installed as party chairman, as a telegenic and confident campaigner, Yudhoyono advanced to the second round of voting to compete with Megawati. In the runoff election, the scope of campaigning was strictly limited, with large rallies prohibited by law. While Megawati pursued a traditional strategy of attempting to coopt the vote blocs of parties that had been eliminated from the race, Yudhoyono instead sought to mobilize the voters directly. As Dagg (2007: 56) summarizes, "The essence of Yudhoyono's strategy was to capitalize on his personal appeal and his reform agenda, as well as on Indonesians' perception that he sought victory by directly responding to their needs. He was portrayed as representing a break from the old model of backroom power brokering, which disenfranchised the people." He defeated Megawati in a landslide.

The reality that Yudhoyono's opponents in 2004 had failed to appreciate was just how much decentralization had reshaped the incentives of local-level elites. Local political and economic imperatives now dictated their loyalties, with no overwhelming incentive to mobilize the personal patronage networks they had painstakingly cultivated in service of their party's presidential candidate. Agents simply had no incentive to cater to the needs of their principals. The then-Golkar chairman later admitted to his shock at seeing the formidable Megawati campaign apparatus being defeated by a candidate backed by a party which held virtually no sway over regional executives or legislatures (Mietzner 2013: 148). Golkar was emblematic of the decline of the vertically integrated patronage machine in Indonesia. Its party leaders simply "failed to capitalise on the presidentialisation trend … [T]hey believed that voters could still be mobilised easily through party machines" (Tomsa 2010: 149). In the end, the election "had come down to a struggle between the status quo, backed by political machines, and reformist populism" with Yudhoyono's populism coming out triumphant (Dagg 2007: 57).

Yudhoyono represented a challenge to the status quo. He was regarded as "clean, democratic, educated, competent and disciplined" (Honna 2012: 473). This image of self-control and competence is not typically associated with populism; indeed according to some conceptualizations, it would rule Yudhoyono out as a populist altogether (Ostiguy 2009). Yudhoyono was certainly not a typical rabble-rousing populist but what matters, according to the organizational conceptualization of populism, is that the appeal of his campaign was thoroughly personalistic. This is illustrated by the substantial discrepancy between support for Yudhoyono and support for the party. Although Yudhoyono won 33.6 percent of the vote in the first round of the presidential election, the PD won only 7.45 percent of the votes in the related legislative election (Hicken 2006b). In fact, most of Yudhoyono's votes in both the first and second rounds in 2004 came from supporters of parties other than his own. Survey evidence analyzed by Liddle and Mujani (2007) suggests that individual leadership rather than party identification or any other socioeconomic criterion was the most important factor in vote choice for president. Individual voter affection for Yudhoyono in 2004 was correlated with exposure to advertisements through the mass media (Mujani, Liddle et al. 2018: 225).

In power, Yudhoyono embraced the strategic use of social policy – cash transfers, health insurance, and rural development – to further cultivate his base of support and to become, at least partially, a more traditionally clientelistic president. Indeed, the Yudhoyono government continued to be heavily influenced by elite interests. The oligarchs of the Suharto era continued to control Indonesia's political economy into the democratic era and Yudhoyono did little to curtail this trend (Fukuoka 2013, Hadiz 2010, Winters 2011: ch. 4). The perception persisted that the government represented interests of the elite, not those of the people. Yet Yudhoyono was sill reelected in 2009. Popular belief in his personal qualities remained high and offset concerns over still-rampant corruption. Following his reelection, Rizal Sukma (2009: 320) wrote that: "many Indonesians admire Yudhoyono for his personal qualities, seeing him as polite, wise, fatherly, well-mannered and calm." The degree of dedication, not to say devotion, of Yudhoyono's support base seems to have been much less intense than is the case for other populist leaders, such as Duterte. In that sense, Yudhoyono might be considered less than fully populist. Indeed, as his second term approached its end, the perception grew that he paid more attention to his personal status than to the practicalities of governing with his popularity consequently declining (Aspinall and Mietzner 2014).

Without a charismatic leader to replace him, the PD was susceptible to outflanking by other populist movements. Both candidates in the 2014 presidential election capitalized on the lack of support for the incumbent PD and on the decline of party machineries in general. As in the Philippines, party identification and party loyalty has only dropped over time (see Figure 3). Party membership fell by around 75 percent between 2004 and 2014. Party identification has fallen by even more, with multiple new personalist electoral vehicles capturing increasing shares of the vote (Muhtadi 2018: 19). Even though the 2008 Presidential Election Law meant that candidates had to be nominated by a party or coalition that won at least 25 percent of the popular vote or 112 (20 percent) of 560 seats of the legislature, just 15 percent of Indonesians felt close to a political party at the time of the 2014 legislative elections (Muhtadi 2018) and only 9 percent by the time of the presidential elections (Mujani, Liddle et al. 2018: 188). As a result, the 2014 campaign would be based heavily on the personalities of the two competing candidates. Indeed, the 2014 presidential election was remarkable in that both of the main candidates were populist, at least to a degree (Aspinall and Mietzner 2014). Prabowo's Gerindra party, and to an extent, the PDI-P, included imagery of the presidential candidates even in local election campaigns (Muhtadi 2018: 24).

Prabowo Subianto is in many ways a classic populist. He is the former son-in-law of former President Suharto and was deeply connected to oligarchic interests in traditional and modern industries (Aspinall 2015). In 2004, he unsuccessfully sought the presidential nomination of Golkar, Suharto's former electoral machine, and in 2009, ran as the vice-presidential partner of Megawati. Unsuccessful, Prabowo founded his own party, Gerindra, which became a personal political vehicle. Mietzner (2014a: 113) writes that "Prabowo, for his part, presented himself as a classic populist strongman, lambasting the weakness and corruption of Indonesia's political class." Despite his oligarchic background, he pitched himself as an "outsider" and a "maverick" (*Al Jazeera English*, 16 July 2014, quoted in Aspinall and Mietzner 2014: 352). Prabowo emulated the imagery of Indonesia's nationalist hero, Sukarno, carefully cultivating a persona of the strongman who could save the country. Aburizal Bakrie, who owns one of the country's major TV stations, TV One, along with another media (and industrial) tycoon, Hary Tanoesoedibjo (formerly with Hanura), joined the Prabowo camp, providing the latter with powerful media forces to compete against his popular opponent (Fukuoka and na Thalang 2014). Prabowo explicitly promised to roll back the constitutional amendments that had provided for the direct elections of subnational government, partially returning Indonesia to the centralism of the Suharto era.

More than Prabowo, Jokowi had come to be seen as a challenger to Indonesia's oligarchy, and his phenomenal popularity as governor of Jakarta forced Megawati to nominate him as the PDI-P's presidential candidate in spite of her own continued interest in the position. Although nominally a member of the PDI-P, Jokowi had only weak interest in or institutional ties to the party (Mietzner 2015). Jokowi in turn went beyond the party leadership to establish direct connections with voters on the basis of a massive grassroots and social-media campaign (Tapsell 2015). In these senses, Jokowi can be considered a populist (Mietzner 2015). However, Jokowi lacks the kind of internal authority over the PDI-P that other populists who have taken over existing parties have generally had. That is, Jokowi has the *external* dimension of charismatic leadership in terms of his relationship with supporters, but not the *internal* dimension of dominance over his movement, as the PDI-P remains a fragmented and clientelistic party over which he has limited control. This may change if Jokowi receives a second term and Megawati loses control over the party, but it leads me to treat Jokowi as a *partial* populist.

Nevertheless, even as a partial populist, Jokowi's charismatic appeals to voters played a significant role in his 2014 election. Even though up to a third of Indonesian voters were offered money for their votes in the lead-up to the election, and even though vote buying impacted behavior for local office, there was no association between vote buying and support in the presidential elections (Muhtadi 2018). The inability of party machines to reliably turn out support for national office has given populist leaders an advantage at that level. Party identification was associated with presidential choice for both Prabowo and Jokowi (Mujani, Liddle et al. 2018: 199–200). However, it has to be recalled that this accounted for less than 10 percent of voters. Moreover, as we lack panel data on voters' past party identification, it is not possible to say whether support for Prabowo and Jokowi respectively drove party identification or the relationship ran in the other direction. Mujani, Liddle et al.'s evidence suggest that it is the former (2018: 217–220). As with Yudhoyono in 2004, affection for both Jokowi and Prabowo was strongly correlated with exposure to advertisements through the mass media (Mujani, Liddle et al. 2018: 225). Most likely, the popularity of the leaders transferred over to their parties.

In sum, since the return of democracy to Indonesia, a sequence of administrative and political decentralizing reforms has gradually weakened the political machines that inherited the New Order state apparatus. Patronage remains *the* central means of securing access to (lower) political office in Indonesia. There is no guarantee that the distribution of patronage will deliver victory, but it is the minimum requirement to have a realistic chance at local office. However, presidential politics are different. Local party branches are so effectively autonomous of central leadership, they have little to gain from devoting scarce patronage resources to mobilize voters in the race for the Presidency (Aspinall 2014b). Successful (and nearly successful) campaigns for the Indonesian presidency have been characterized by their appreciation of the persistent fragmentation between national and subnational politics. Yudhoyono, Prabowo, and to an extent Jokowi embraced populist mobilizational strategies in which they developed direct emotional ties with voters that brought them to power (or close to it) irrespective of the dynamics of subnational patronage politics.

Although personalistic parties have been common in Thailand, full-blown populism has been relatively unusual. For instance, the Chart Pattana Party (CPP), Social Action, and New Aspiration were all associated with particular party leaders – usually their founders. Yet most of them depended for their electoral support on building up coalitions of local rural notables, deploying patronage to mobilize the vote. Prachakorn Thai (PTP) and Muan Chon (MCP) parties followed the same approach, but instead directed their particularistic appeals toward urban groups. Such parties are thus more appropriately classified as clientelistic.

Populism in Thailand is virtually synonymous with the parties of Thaksin Shinawatra, the Thai Rak Thai (TRT) and the Pheu Thai Party (PTP). Prior to Thaksin's emergence on the political scene in the late 1990s, Thai politics had been characterized by inter-elite factionalism rather than inter-party competition. The 1997 Constitution had been intended to reduce the role of rural elites and to promote stronger and more nationally focused parties (Hicken 2006a), albeit ones that catered to the interests of the elite that surrounded the ruling nexus of the monarchy, the military, and the business elite. By having a (partial) party list voting system with a high minimum threshold, the idea was that parties would have to appeal on the grounds of policy.

In a sense, the reforms were successful (Hicken 2006b). They pushed political leaders to focus on policy-based appeals. However, the institutional reforms did not internally transform parties into bureaucratically organized entities with systematic rules, procedures, and lines of authority – rather they remained personalistic and fragmented; similarly the reforms did not suddenly create parties with deeply institutionalized ties to civil society organizations. At the same time, the Asian Financial Crisis of 1997 badly damaged the reputations of the Democratic Party and New Aspiration parties, which had come to be the country's predominant political machines. As a result, what emerged in Thailand in the late 1990s was what McCargo (1997) called the "electoral professional party." Such parties make direct appeals to the electorate, without any concern for formal party structures and depend primarily on "a highly marketable leader" (McCargo and Patthamānan 2005: 78). This represented "a new mode of Thai party in which the leadership sought to establish a direct connection with voters through the media and through a variety of marketing techniques" (McCargo and Patthamānan 2005: 77). In short, rather than creating bureaucratic parties, the reforms created the conditions for charismatic campaigners to appeal directly to the people with only a limited party organization.

For some observers, Thaksin and his Thai Rak Thai (TRT) party didn't begin as a populist movement (Hawkins and Selway 2017, Phongpaichit and Baker 2008). Thaksin's populism is usually linked to the policy platform he set out during his first period of government – the three-point plan of 2001 which included cheap health care, fund pools for villages, and debt relief for rural farmers. Others date Thaksin's turn to populism even later when he explicitly began to court the support of poorer rural voters (Hawkins and Selway 2017). It is true that Thaksin only shifted from extremely vague policies and more modest framing in the late 1990s toward inflammatory fanning of rural sentiments in the mid-2000s, but I argue that it is a mistake not to see Thaksin's entire rise in terms of populism.

As early as his 1999 autobiography, Thaksin derided the bickering and factionalism of "professional politicians" (Phongpaichit and Baker 2009: 64); echoing the rhetoric of many other populists around the world, he called for a new post-partisan era, in which the people would unite in common purpose. Privately, Thaksin disdained the voting populace (McCargo and Patthamānan 2005: 10). Publically, however, by this time, and certainly by the time of the 2001 elections, Thaksin had seen the potential of a personalistic form of mass mobilization. Thaksin promised redistribution but perhaps as important, he pitched himself as an alternative to the political establishment. Thaksin drew on his past in the Thai police and on his contemporary position as a high-flying CEO to portray an image of a strong leader who was beholden to no special interests (McCargo and Patthamānan 2005: 5).

The TRT would come to be the most prominent of the new group of "professional electoral parties" described by McCargo (1997). The fact that some of its founding members were prominent academics gave the TRT some distinction, and suggested it might be guided by reformist policies; by the end of its first year, however, it looked very much like a party built around business networks close to the state. What would be distinctive about the TRT was not primarily its policy platform but Thaksin's status as one of the country's most successful businessmen and his ability to appeal to voters directly. Fitting precisely the conceptualization of populist mobilization described in Section 2, the TRT "sought to bypass the existing linkages between ordinary voters and local politicians and MPs, creating a direct connection between the electorate and the government," itself personified by Thaksin (McCargo and Patthamānan 2005: 110). The CEO has been a frequent populist figure in the Americas, both north and south. Like Donald Trump, Thaksin could argue that he *personally* would fix the Thai economy; he could make the tough decisions and cut through the special interests; he could put Thailand's interests first in the same way that he had done for Shin Corp. Thaksin was portrayed by his supporters as a "white knight" who alone could rescue Thailand from its malaise (McCargo and Patthamānan 2005: 15).

The TRT, like other populist parties in clientelistic systems such as Duterte's LDP-Laban in the Philippines, did incorporate some pre-existing political factions. Such factions, or localized patron–client networks, are characterized in Thailand, as elsewhere, by an ability to move from one coalition to another, depending on the direction of the political winds. Thaksin's ability to dominate the party-list vote in 2001 through his direct, charismatic appeals to the electorate meant that he would be in prime position to form a government for some time to come. Bandwagoning with the TRT made perfect sense for faction leaders, even if the TRT was nominally "anti-faction." Like the Bharatiya Janata Party (BJP) under Narendra Modi in India, the TRT combined direct top down appeals from its leader with old-style patronage. This is suggested in part by the rural concentration in the TRT's support. It gained the majority of its vote share in those rural districts where patronage politics had prevailed (Phongpaichit and Baker 2009). Ultimately, Thaksin looked to create a "super-party" that would effectively subsume all existing parties within his own (McCargo and Patthamānan 2005: 106). Chart Pattana and Chart Thai were effectively incorporated into the TRT in 2004.

Thaksin also looked to dominate the media space, in part for financial reasons, but also for political ones. By controlling what the public saw and heard, he could retain his direct link to them. Phongpaichit and Baker (2008: 71) write:

> First, he manufactured a public presence significantly greater than that attempted by any previous Thai prime minister, primarily by using state-owned media now under his control. He launched a weekly radio show in which he talked to the nation for an hour about his activities and his thoughts on issues of the day. He dominated the daily television news and also appeared in several special programmes, including an evening chat show in which he lamented his predecessors' handling of the economy.

Direct media links, in other words, were crucial to the consolidation of TRT support. The TRT claimed to have a mass membership base of some 8 million by 2000. However, membership was not the result of deep social ties to the party and its agenda but of money politics (Nelson 2001). In reality, the institutional base of the TRT was very limited. Local branches had little influence on the party's platform and did little to augment its electoral support. The TRT was internally leader-centric, even authoritarian, "an organization centred entirely around a single man" (McCargo and Patthamānan 2005: 110). It was, in short, Thaksin's party. It won because of Thaksin.

Almost from the moment of his election triumph, Thaksin found himself at odds with constitutional constraints on his authority. In running for Prime Minister, Thaksin was technically in violation of a minor provision of the Constitution that forbade him from standing for election on account of his failure to disclose his assets while deputy prime minister in a previous government. Thaksin and his supporters openly pressured the judiciary to respect the will of the people. No doubt, Thaksin was the democratic (i.e., majority) choice. However, his willingness to override institutional rules in the name of the people was telling (McCargo and Patthamānan 2005: 15–16). McCargo and

Patthamānan (2005: 16) write: "Thaksin's approach to the new institutions was to penetrate them, politicize them and to subordinate them to his own will and purposes." As I discuss in the conclusion, this even extended to launching an extrajudicial war on drugs of his own, albeit one on a smaller scale than that of Duterte in the Philippines.

Thaksin, in short, deeply personalized power in a way that challenged vested interests, not least those associated with state-military-business networks. Thaksin was removed from power in a military coup in 2006, and the TRT banned. His personal influence has persisted in spite of his self-imposed exile (Thaksin was sentenced to two years in prison in absentia for abuse of power). His younger sister, Yingluck Shinawatra led the TRT's successor party, the PTP, to victory in 2011, before it too was ousted because of political unrest in which monarchist, nationalist, and urbanite "yellows" squared off against rural Thaksin-supporting "reds" through 2013. Although Thai politics has become increasingly divided over policy, this has not meant the formation of a bureaucratic party system but one polarized between a personalist political vehicle that swamped the rural patronage party machines and a coalition of urban middle-classes and elites connected to the administrative-military-monarchy network. The new Constitution, ratified in 2017, may limit the scope for a populist leader to actually control the government. It does so, however, by placing severe limits on the freedom of Thai democracy. Given the lack of bureaucratically organized parties across the political spectrum, populism is thus likely to remain a persistent latent threat that could re-emerge if restrictions on mobilization are lifted.

The rise of Thaksin to power shares several notable characteristics with the successful campaigns of populists elsewhere in the region. Thaksin, like other populists, was the dominant charismatic leader of his political movement. Even though institutional reforms were put in place in 1997in order to strengthen political parties, leadership came to be the crucial determinant of political behavior for most voters. The same has been true in Indonesia and the Philippines, which have seen a string of populist leaders with only weakly institutionalized, if not non-existent, party structures behind them. Even if attached to local politicians through ties of patronage, voters are heavily swayed by direct personal appeals when it comes to choosing their nation's leader. Populists across the region have drawn on their personal credibility, whether as former military men or successful businessmen, to oppose the corruption of the so-called establishment – of which, in reality, many of them were a part.

We are only beginning to understand the individual level logic behind voters' support for charismatic leaders. Given the success of populist candidates elsewhere in recent years, not least in the United States, however, there is little reason to think that the appeal of populism is unique to Southeast Asian voters, and any putative values they are alleged to hold. Although we do not have complete survey data across the region, support for populist candidates does not appear to be driven by any authoritarian or other personality dispositions. Similarly, the class basis of support for populist candidates is also diverse. Some, like Thaksin, obtained support mostly from a frustrated middle peasantry; others like Duterte, from both the poor and the wealthy and urban middle class. Rather, what unites supporters of populist candidates is their general lack of loyalty toward political parties. This fickleness, while it frequently brings populists to power, further undermines party institutionalization, and potentially with it, democracy itself. I take this issue up in the final section.

6 Conclusion: Populism and Democracy

Populist leaders attempt to forge direct or unmediated relationships with their followers, whether through mass rallies, mass media, or social media tools such as Twitter. This antipathy toward intermediation translates into the erosion of checks and balances on executive power when populists gain office. In places such as Rodrigo Duterte's Philippines and Thaksin's Thailand, the erosion of the rule of law has had devastating implications for human rights. While populists often mobilize parts of the population previously ignored by established parties, they also often look to demobilize their opponents. Populism in Southeast Asia, as elsewhere, has thus had not had a positive effect on democracy. Given the persistent absence of bureaucratic parties in the region, the prospect of further democratic erosion remains high.

The antagonism between populism and democracy is no coincidence and it is not unique to Southeast Asia. Rather, in seeking to establish and maintain a *direct* relationship to supporters, populists are inherently driven to erode the intermediary institutions that might get in the way (Urbinati 2015); this includes parties, courts, legislatures, the press, the academy, or any other agency that purports to challenge the populist's singular legitimacy. Moreover, the lack of formal or informal internal party constraints on populist leaders further frees them from adhering to democratic rules of the game (Kenny 2018). Indeed, a growing body of empirical research now demonstrates that populists erode democracy across most measurable dimensions (Allred, Hawkins et al. 2015, Houle and Kenny 2018, Huber and Schimpf 2016, Kenny 2017: ch. 2, Kenny 2018).

Populist rule in the region can certainly tend toward the authoritarian. In power, Duterte has waged a violent campaign against drug-related criminality, with estimates of the number of those killed in the first 18 months of his presidency running as high as 12,000. Although not on this scale, Thaksin's own "war" against crime in 2003 and 2004 left some 2,000 dead in the first three months.[13] Even if the numbers were lower than those in the Philippines, the manner of killings was often more spectacular – in restaurants, the middle of main roads, and in middle-class gated communities. The language used by Thaksin and cabinet members had strong resonances with that of Duterte as well. In the same period, civil society leaders, environmentalists, and others were disappeared, killed, or threatened. Notably, however, the targets were generally of a higher socio-economic status than the poor being shot dead in Manila's slums. This dimension of Thaksin's police state may have contributed to his declining support among the middle class in favour of the military, the so-called "tank liberals" (Ungpakorn 2007), while Duterte's support remains most robust among the well-to-do.

Given the antipathy between populism and democracy, it may come as a surprise that some of populism's staunchest opponents in Southeast Asia and elsewhere have been the military, who after all, have been no friends of democracy themselves. However, if we appreciate that democracy in Southeast Asia (as in other regions such as Latin America and the Middle East) has created the conditions in which populists thrive, this puzzle is more easily addressed. Rather than allow a populist outsider to come to power and undermine the autonomy of the military, whether through personnel changes or even the creation of parallel armed institutions, militaries and their supporters in the bureaucracy and the judiciary have stepped in to take control themselves. The Thai case is especially illustrative. Thaksin's ability to entrench his rule was constrained by the country's apex court that played a significant role in defending the interest of the monarchy and the military against the TRT and its reincarnations and appendages. Thaksin had the police on his side from the beginning, dominated the legislature, and could fashion ostensibly independent agencies under the 1997 constitution to suit his interests. The courts were distinct, however. Indeed, this was recognized in the language from the TRT – which accused its opponents of "judicial coup"-making – and which grew louder at each instance of a decision against them. The courts were intermediary institutions that Thaksin did not have the capacity to erode. They were not susceptible to the kinds of political interventions that characterize populist judicial politics elsewhere, not least the Philippines, and the anti-Thaksin forces worked through the superior judiciary with full effect. This of course,

---

[13] Seth Mydans, "A wave of drug killings is linked to police," *The New York Times*, 8 April 2003, www.nytimes.com/2003/04/08/world/a-wave-of-drug-killings-is-linked-to-thai-police.html, accessed 23 August 2018.

did not mean a triumph of liberalism or anything like it. The courts defended, indeed promoted, a political order that was far less than democratic (Connors and Hewison 2008).

Although Yudhoyono and Jokowi have not directly eroded democracy to the same extent as Duterte or Thaksin, it would be premature to suggest that there is something fundamentally different about the circumstances that give rise to these more "moderate" cases of populist rule. As Presidents, both Yudhoyono and Jokowi have ruled in conjunction with coalitions in the People's Representative Council, which may have constrained their personalization of power in a way not possible in parliamentary Thailand. Yet neither Yudhoyono nor Jokowi made much attempt to move their parties in a more bureaucratic direction. Rather their populist strategies provide a strong signal that political power in Indonesia does not depend on party building. Moreover, it is worth noting that Prabowo Subianto came very close to winning the 2014 presidential election and is gearing up for another run in 2019. A former general, Prabowo has never made much secret of his authoritarian leanings. His Gerindra party manifesto even stated "The political system that has been heading in the direction of liberal democracy since the reformasi era needs to be corrected" (Aspinall 2015: 19). Prabowo does not seem to have abandoned these beliefs and the implicit threat he poses to Indonesia's democracy remains. Moreover, even Jokowi, once regarded as a more "moderate" populist (Mietzner 2015), has taken steps to erode the organizational capacity of rival, especially Islamist, political parties, leading Mietzner (2018: 263) to now conclude that Jokowi has "eroded rather than bolstered the democratic status quo." Whether the Indonesian judicial system has the capacity or desire to prevent such back-sliding remains an open question. Ironically, in the Indonesian case, it may the very multiplicity of competing oligarchic interests, even if they are separately anti-democratic, that preserves a democratic status quo of sorts.

What the Southeast Asian cases reveal is a persistent three-way tension between patronage-based democracy, populism, and military-authoritarian centralism. Advocates of liberal democracy in the region are thus in some ways damned if they do and damned if they don't. For those who remember the brutality of left and right wing authoritarian governments that governed much of the world in the second half of the twentieth century, it can seem hard to imagine any reasonable alternative to liberal democracy. One of the great virtues of contemporary liberalism is the central place it affords to toleration or pluralism (Fawcett 2014). Yet liberal democracy seems to work only when coherent bureaucratic political parties exist to manage it (Dalton, Farrell et al. 2011). As E. E. Schattschneider (1942) put it, democracy may be "unthinkable" without parties. Strong parties, clearly aligned with underlying interest groups, whether of the left or right, underpinned the glory days of post-war Western European democracy. Yet even in the West, such parties have become progressively weaker in recent decades (Mair 2013), opening up the space for populist outsiders to make significant electoral inroads. Populism is thus as much a *symptom* as a *cause* of weak democracy, and weak parties.

Critically, for the purposes of this book, outside Western Europe and North America, parties have been even weaker. Low levels of civil society organization, high levels of inequality, and infrastructurally weak states have meant that following the temporarily unifying nationalist effect of anti-colonial independence movements, most parties have developed on the basis of contingent alliances between patronage-based political factions. Democrats in Southeast Asia thus have to contend not only with the socioeconomic and technological changes that have weakened bureaucratic parties everywhere, but also with their particular disadvantageous historical legacies. This does not mean we need to accept the Huntingtonian view that developing countries are "not ready" for democracy (Huntington 2006); rather it means that to the extent that liberal democracy remains a worthy goal – as Churchill put it, "the worst form of government except all the others that have been tried" – it means at the same time as building bureaucratic parties, democrats need to find ways of fostering robust, open, and non-sectarian civil societies, developing effective state institutions, and addressing socioeconomic inequalities.

References

Abinales, P. N. (2003). Progressive-machine conflict in early-twentieth century U.S. politics and colonial state building in the Philippines. In *The American Colonial State in the Philippines: Global Perspectives*, J. Go and A. L. Foster (eds.). Durham, NC: Duke University Press.

Achen, C. H. and L. M. Bartels (2016). *Democracy for Realists: Why Elections Do Not Produce Responsive Government*. Princeton, NJ, Princeton University Press.

Akkerman, A., C. Mudde and A. Zaslove (2013). "How populist are the people? Measuring populist attitudes in voters." *Comparative Political Studies* 47(9): 1324–1353.

Allred, N., K. A. Hawkins and S. P. Ruth (2015). The Impact of Populism on Liberal Democracy. Paper presented at the 8th Congreso de la Asociación Latinoamericana de Ciencia Política. Lima, Peru.

Arghiros, D. (2001). *Democracy, Development and Decentralization in Provincial Thailand*. Richmond: Curzon.

Aspinall, E. (2005). "Elections and the normalization of politics in Indonesia." *South East Asia Research* 13(2): 117–156.

Aspinall, E. (2013a). How Indonesia survived: Comparative perspectives on state disintegration and endurance. In *Democracy and Islam in Indonesia.*, A. Stepan and M. Kunkler (eds.). New York: Columbia University Press, pp. 126–148.

Aspinall, E. (2013b). "The triumph of capital? Class politics and Indonesian Democratisation." *Journal of Contemporary Asia* 43(2): 226–242.

Aspinall, E. (2014a). "Parliament and patronage." *Journal of Democracy* 25 (4): 96–110.

Aspinall, E. (2014b). "When brokers betray: Clientelism, social networks, and electoral politics in Indonesia." *Critical Asian Studies* 46(4): 545–570.

Aspinall, E. (2015). "Oligarchic populism: Prabowo Subianto's challenge to Indonesian democracy." *Indonesia* 99(1): 1–28.

Aspinall, E. and W. Berenschot (forthcoming). *Democracy for Sale: Elections, Clientelism, and the State in Indonesia*. Ithaca, NY: Cornell University Press.

Aspinall, E., M. Davidson, A. Hicken and M. Weiss (2016). "Local machines and vote brokerage in the Philippines." *Contemporary Southeast Asia* 38(2): 191–196.

Aspinall, E., M. Davidson, A. Hicken and M. Weiss (2015). Inducement or Entry Ticket? Broker Networks and Vote Buying in Indonesia. Paper presented at the annual meeting of the American Political Science Association, San Francisco.

Aspinall, E. and M. Mietzner (2014). "Indonesian politics in 2014: Democracy's close call." *Bulletin of Indonesian Economic Studies* 50(3): 347–369.

Autor, D., D. Dorn, G. Hanson and K. Majlesi (2016). Importing Political Polarization? Unpublished manuscript, Massachusetts Institute of Technology.

Baker, C. J. and P. Phongpaichit (2014). *A History of Thailand*. Cambridge : Cambridge University Press.

Bakker, B. N., M. Rooduijn and G. Schumacher (2016). "The psychological roots of populist voting: Evidence from the United States, the Netherlands and Germany." *European Journal of Political Research* 55(2): 302–320.

Barr, R. R. (2009). "Populists, outsiders and anti-establishment politics." *Party Politics* 15(1): 29–48.

Benoit, K., D. Conway, B. E. Lauderdale, M. Laver and S. Mikhaylov (2016). "Crowd-sourced text analysis: Reproducible and agile production of political data." *American Political Science Review* 110(2): 278–295.

Bensman, J. and M. Givant (1975). "Charisma and modernity: The use and abuse of a concept." *Social Research* 42(4): 570–614.

Berenschot, W. (2010). "Everyday mediation: The politics of public service delivery in Gujarat, India." *Development and Change* 41(5): 883–905.

Boix, C. (1999). "Setting the rules of the game: the choice of electoral systems in advanced democracies." *American Political Science Review* 93(03): 609–624.

Bolongaita, E. P. (1999). "The Philippines: Consolidating democracy in difficult times." *Southeast Asian Affairs*: 237–252.

Booth, A. (1999). "Initial conditions and miraculous growth: Why is South East Asia different from Taiwan and South Korea?" *World Development* 27 (2): 301–321.

Booth, A. (2014). Before the "big bang": Decentralization debates and practice in Indonesia, 1949–99. In *Regional Dynamics in a Decentralized Indonesia*, H. Hill (ed.). Singapore: Institute of Southeast Asian Studies, pp. 25–44.

Booth, A. (2016). *Economic Change in Modern Indonesia: Colonial and Post-Colonial Comparisons*. Cambridge: Cambridge University Press.

Bornschier, S. (2010). *Cleavage Politics and the Populist Right: The New Cultural Conflict in Western Europe*. Philadelphia, PA: Temple University Press.

Brands, H. W. (1992). *Bound to Empire: the United States and the Philippines*. New York: Oxford University Press.

Buehler, M. (2010). Decentralisation and local democracy in Indonesia: the marginalisation of the public sphere. In *Problems of Democratisation in*

Indonesia: Elections, Institutions, and Society, E. Aspinall and M. Mietzner (eds.). Singapore: Institute of Southeast Asian Studies, pp. 267–285.

Buehler, M. (2014). Elite competition and changing state–society relations: Shari'a policymaking in Indonesia. In *Beyond Oligarchy: Wealth, Power, and Contemporary Indonesian Politics*, M. Ford and T. Pepinsky (eds.). Ithaca: Cornell Southeast Asia Program Publications, pp. 157–176.

Calimbahin, C. (2009). The Promise and Pathology of Democracy: The Commission on Elections of the Philippines. PhD Dissertation, University of Wisconsin-Madison.

Callahan, W. A. and D. McCargo (1996). "Vote-buying in Thailand's northeast: The July 1995 general election." *Asian Survey* 36(4): 376–392.

Canovan, M. (1999). "Trust the people! Populism and the two faces of democracy." *Political Studies* 47(1): 2–16.

Caramani, D. (2004). *The Nationalization of Politics: The Formation of National Electorates and Party Systems in Western Europe*. Cambridge: Cambridge University Press.

Carnegie, P. J. (2008). "Democratization and decentralization in post-Soeharto Indonesia: Understanding transition dynamics." *Pacific Affairs* 81(4): 515–525.

Case, W. (2017). *Populist Threats and Democracy's Fate in Southeast Asia: Thailand, the Philippines, and Indonesia*. New York: Routledge.

Casiple, R. C. (2016). "The Duterte presidency as a phenomenon." *Contemporary Southeast Asia: A Journal of International and Strategic Affairs* 38(2): 179–184.

Chambers, P. (2008). "Factions, parties and the durability of parliaments, coalitions and cabinets: The case of Thailand (1979 – 2001)." *Party Politics* 14(3): 299–323.

Chandra, K. (2004). *Why Ethnic Parties Succeed: Patronage and Ethnic Head Counts in India*. New York, Cambridge University Press.

Co, E. E. A., J. V. Tigno, M. E. J. Lao, and M. A. Sayo (2005). *Philippine Democracy Assessment: Free and Fair Elections and the Democratic Role of Political Parties*. Metro Manila: Friedrich Ebert Stiftung and National College of Public Administration and Governance, University of the Philippines.

Cohen, G. L. (2003). "Party over policy: The dominating impact of group influence on political beliefs." *Journal of Personality and Social Psychology* 85(5): 808–822.

Collier, R. B. and D. Collier (2002). *Shaping the Political Arena: Critical Junctures, the Labor Movement, and Regime Dynamics in Latin America*. South Bend, IN: Notre Dame Press.

Connors, M. K. and K. Hewison (2008). "Introduction: Thailand and the "good coup."" *Journal of Contemporary Asia* 38(1): 1–10.

Constantino, R. and L. R. Constantino (1975). *A History of the Philippines: From the Spanish Colonization to the Second World War*. New York: Monthly Review Press.

Crouch, H. (1985). *Economic Change, Social Structure and the Political System in Southeast Asia: Philippine Development Compared with the Other ASEAN Countries*. Singapore: Institute of Southeast Asian Studies.

Cullather, N. (1993). "America's boy? Ramon Magsaysay and the illusion of influence." *Pacific Historical Review* 62(3): 305–338.

Cullinane, M. (1989). *Ilustrado Politics: Filipino Elite Responses to American Rule, 1898–1908*, Manila: Ateneo de Manila University Press.

Curato, N. (2017). "Flirting with authoritarian fantasies? Rodrigo Duterte and the new terms of Philippine populism." *Journal of Contemporary Asia* 47 (1): 142–153.

Cusack, T. R., T. Iversen and D. Soskice (2007). "Economic interests and the origins of electoral systems." *American Political Science Review* 101(3): 373–391.

Dagg, C. J. (2007). "The 2004 elections in Indonesia: Political reform and democratisation." *Asia Pacific Viewpoint* 48(1): 47–59.

Dalton, R. J., D. M. Farrell and I. McAllister (2011). *Political Parties and Democratic Linkage: How Parties Organize Democracy*. Oxford: Oxford University Press.

Dalton, R. J. and M. P. Wattenberg (2000). *Parties without Partisans: Political Change in Advanced Industrial Democracies*. Oxford: Oxford University Press.

De Castro, R. C. (2007). "The 1997 Asian financial crisis and the revival of populism/neo-populism in 21st century Philippine politics." *Asian Survey* 47 (6): 930–951.

Di Tella, T. (1965). Populism and reform in Latin America. In *Obstacles to Change in Latin America*, C. Veliz (ed.). London: Oxford University Press.

Doner, R. F. (2009). *The Politics of Uneven Development: Thailand's Economic Growth in Comparative Perspective*. New York: Cambridge University Press.

Doyle, D. (2011). "The legitimacy of political institutions." *Comparative Political Studies* 44(11): 1447–1473.

Dustmann, C., B. Eichengreen, S. Otten, A. Sapir, G. Tabellini and G. Zoega (2017). *Europe's Trust Deficit: Causes and Remedies*. London: CEPR Press.

Eisenstadt, S. N. (1973). *Traditional Patrimonialism and Modern Neopatrimonialism*. Beverly Hills, CA: Sage Publications.

Eisenstadt, S. N. and L. Roniger (1980). "Patron-client relations as a model of structuring social exchange." *Comparative Studies in Society and History* 22(1): 42–77.

Evans, G. and K. Chzhen (2013). "Explaining voters' defection from Labour over the 2005–10 electoral cycle: Leadership, economics and the rising importance of ommigration." *Political Studies* 61(1 suppl): 138–157.

Fawcett, E. (2014). *Liberalism: The Life of an Idea*. Princeton, NJ: Princeton University Press.

Feith, H. (2007 [1962]). *The Decline of Constitutional Democracy in Indonesia*. Jakarta: Equinox Pub.

Feith, H. and L. Castles (1970). *Indonesian Political Thinking: 1945–1965*. Ithaca, NY: Cornell University Press.

Fukuoka, Y. (2013). "Indonesia's 'democratic transition' revisited: A clientelist model of political transition." *Democratization* 20(6): 991–1013.

Fukuoka, Y. and C. na Thalang (2014). "The legislative and presidential elections in Indonesia in 2014." *Electoral Studies* 36: 230–235.

Garrido, M. (2013). "The ideology of the dual city: The modernist ethic in the corporate development of Makati City, Metro Manila." *International Journal of Urban and Regional Research* 37(1): 165–185.

Germani, G. (1978). *Authoritarianism, Fascism, and National Populism*. New Brunswick, NJ, Transaction Books.

Green, D. P., B. Palmquist and E. Schickler (2002). *Partisan Hearts and Minds: Political Parties and the Social Identities of Voters*. New Haven, CT: Yale University Press.

Hadiz, V. R. (2010). *Localising Power in Post-Authoritarian Indonesia: A Southeast Asia Perspective*. Stanford, CA, Stanford University Press.

Hadiz, V. R. (2016). *Islamic Populism in Indonesia and the Middle East*. Cambridge, UK: Cambridge University Press.

Hart, D. V. (1953). "Magsaysay: Philippine candidate." *Far Eastern Survey* 22(6): 67–70.

Hawkins, K. and C. Rovira Kaltwasser (2018). Introduction – Concept, theory, and method. In *The Ideational Approach to Populism: Concept, Theory, and Analysis*, K. Hawkins, R. E. Carlin, L. Littvay and C. Rovira Kaltwasser (eds.). New York: Routledge.

Hawkins, K. and J. Selway (2017). "Thaksin the Populist?" *Chinese Political Science Review* 2(3): 372–394.

Hedman, E.-L. E. (2001). "The spectre of populism in Philippine politics and society: Artista, masa, Eraption!" *South East Asia Research* 9(1): 5–44.

Hellmann, O. (2017). Populism in East Asia. In *The Oxford Handbook of Populism*, C. B. Rovira Kaltwasser, P. A. Taggart, P. Ochoa Espejo and P. Ostiguy (eds.). New York: Oxford University Press.

Hewison, K. (2000). "Resisting globalization: A study of localism in Thailand." *The Pacific Review* 13(2): 279–296.

Hicken, A. (2002). The market for votes in Thailand. Paper presented at the international conference, Trading Political Rights: The Comparative Politics of Vote Buying. Center for International Studies, MIT.

Hicken, A. (2006a). "Party fabrication: Constitutional reform and the rise of Thai Rak Thai." *Journal of East Asian Studies* 6(3): 381–407.

Hicken, A. (2006b). "Stuck in the mud: Parties and party systems in democratic Southeast Asia." *Taiwan Journal of Democracy* 2(2): 23–46.

Hicken, A. (2009). *Building Party Systems in Developing Democracies*. New York: Cambridge University Press.

Hicken, A. (2011). "Clientelism." *Annual Review of Political Science* 14: 289–310.

Hicken, A. and E. M. Kuhonta, Eds. (2014). *Party System Institutionalization in Southeast Asia*. New York: Cambridge University Press.

Hoffer, E. (1951). *The True Believer: Thoughts on the Nature of Mass Movements*. New York: Harper.

Holmes, R. (2016). "The Dark Side of Electoralism: Opinion Polls and Voting in the 2016 Philippine Presidential Election." *Journal of Current Southeast Asian Affairs* 35(3): 15–38.

Honna, J. (2012). "Inside the Democrat Party: Power, politics and conflict in Indonesia's presidential party." *South East Asia Research* 20(4): 473–489.

Houle, C. and P. D. Kenny (2018). "The political and economic consequences of populist rule in Latin America." *Government and Opposition* 53(2): 256–287.

Huber, R. A. and C. H. Schimpf (2015). "Friend or Foe? Testing the Influence of Populism on Democratic Quality in Latin America." *Political Studies* 64(4): 872–889.

Huntington, S. P. (2006). *Political Order in Changing Societies*. New Haven, CT: Yale University Press.

Hutchcroft, P. D. (1991). "Oligarchs and cronies in the Philippine state the politics of patrimonial plunder." *World Politics* 43(3): 414–450.

Hutchcroft, P. D. (1998). *Booty Capitalism: The Politics of banking in the Philippines*. Ithaca, NY: Cornell University Press.

Hutchcroft, P. D. (1999). "After the fall: Prospects for political and institutional reform in post-crisis Thailand and the Philippines." *Government and Opposition* 34(4): 473–497.

Hutchcroft, P. D. (2014). Linking capital and the countryside: Patronage and clientelism in Japan, Thailand, and the Philippines. In *Clientelism, Social Policy, and the Quality of Democracy*, D. Abente Brun and L. J. Diamond (eds.). Baltimore: Johns Hopkins University Press, pp. 174–203.

Hutchcroft, P. D. and J. Rocamora (2003). "Strong demands and weak institutions: The origins and evolution of the democratic deficit in the Philippines." *Journal of East Asian Studies* 3: 259–292.

Hynd, E. (2017). Patterns of Political Party Competition, Dominance and Institutionalism: The Case of Timor-Leste. PhD Dissertation, Australian National University.

Inglehart, R. and P. Norris (2017). "Trump and the populist authoritarian parties: The silent revolution in reverse." *Perspectives on Politics* 15(2): 443–454.

Ionescu, G. and E. Gellner, Eds. (1969). *Populism: Its Meaning and National Characteristics*. New York: Macmillan.

Johnson, D. W. (2016). *Democracy for Hire: A History of American Political Consulting*. New York: Oxford University Press.

Judis, J. B. (2016). *The Populist Explosion: How the Great Recession Transformed American and European Politics*. New York: Columbia Global Reports.

Karnow, S. (1990). *In Our Image: America's Empire in the Philippines*. New York: Century.

Kaufmann, E. (2017). "Levels or changes?: Ethnic context, immigration and the UK Independence Party vote." *Electoral Studies* 48: 57–69.

Kenny, P. D. (2015a). "Colonial rule, decolonisation, and corruption in India." *Commonwealth & Comparative Politics* 53(4): 401–427.

Kenny, P. D. (2015b). "The origins of patronage democracy: State building, centrifugalism, and decolonization." *British Journal of Political Science* 45(1): 141–171.

Kenny, P. D. (2017). *Populism and Patronage: Why Populists Win Elections in India, Asia, and Beyond*. Oxford; New York: Oxford University Press.

Kenny, P. D. (2018). "The Enemy of the People": Populists and Press Freedom. Unpublished manuscript, Australian National University.

Kenny, P. D. and R. Holmes (2018). A New Penal Populism? Rodrigo Duterte and the War on Drugs in the Philippines. Paper presented at the World Congress of the International Political Science Association. Brisbane.

Kerkvliet, B. J. (1977). *The Huk Rebellion: A study of Peasant Revolt in the Philippines*. Berkeley: University of California Press.

Kinder, D. R. and N. P. Kalmoe (2017). *Neither Liberal nor Conservative: Ideological Innocence in the American Public*. Chicago; London: University of Chicago Press.

Kitschelt, H. (2000). "Linkages between citizens and politicians in democratic polities." *Comparative Political Studies* 33(6–7): 845–879.

Krastev, I. (2007). "The strange death of the liberal consensus." *Journal of Democracy* 18(4): 56–63.

Kuo, D. (2018). *Clientelism, Capitalism, and Democracy: The Rise of Programmatic Politics in the United States and Britain*. New York: Cambridge University Press.

Landé, C. (1968). "Parties and politics in the Philippines." *Asian Survey* 8(9): 725–747.

Liddle, R. W. and S. Mujani (2007). "Leadership, party, and religion: Explaining voting behavior in Indonesia." *Comparative Political Studies* 40(7): 832–857.

Lipset, S. M. and S. Rokkan (1967). *Party Systems and Voter Alignments: CrossNnational Perspectives*. New York; Free Press.

Lupu, N. (2016). *Party Brands in Crisis: Partisanship, Brand Dilution, and the Breakdown of Political Parties in Latin America*. New York: Cambridge University Press.

MacIntyre, A. J. (1991). *Business and Politics in Indonesia*. North Sydney: Allen & Unwin.

Mair, P. (2013). *Ruling the Void: The Hollowing of Western Democracy*. London: Verso.

McCargo, D. (1997). Thailand's political parties: Real, authentic, and actual. In *Political Change in Thailand: Democracy and Participation*, K. Hewison (ed.). London; New York: Routledge.

McCargo, D. (2005). "Network monarchy and legitimacy crises in Thailand." *The Pacific Review* 18(4): 499–519.

McCargo, D. and U. Patthamānan (2005). *The Thaksinization of Thailand*. Copenhagen: NIAS Press.

McCoy, A. W. (1981). The Philippines: Independence without decolonization. In *Asia: The Winning of Independence*, R. Jeffrey (ed.). New York: St. Martin's Press.

McCoy, A. W. (1989). Quezon's commonwealth: The emergence of Philippine authoritarianism. In *Philippine Colonial Democracy*, R. R. Paredes (ed.). Manila: Ateneo de Manila University Press.

McCoy, A. W. (2009a). Preface: The Philippine oligarchy at the turn of the twenty-first century. In *An Anarchy of Families: State and Family in the Philippines*. A. W. McCoy (ed.). Madison: University of Wisconsin Press, pp. xi–xxxii.

McCoy, A. W. (2009b). "An anarchy of families": The historiography of state and family in the Philippines. In *An Anarchy of Families: State and Family in the Philippines*, A. W. McCoy (ed.). Madison: University of Wisconsin Press, pp. 1–32.

McCoy, A. W. (2017). "Global populism: A lineage of Filipino strongmen from Quezon to Marcos and Duterte." *Kasarinlan: Philippine Journal of Third World Studies* 32(1–2): 7–54.

McVey, R. T. (1965). *The Rise of Indonesian Communism*. Ithaca: Cornell University Press.

Mietzner, M. (2013). *Money, Power and Ideology: Political Parties in Post-Authoritarian Indonesia*. Singapore: Institute of Southeast Asian Studies.

Mietzner, M. (2014a). "How Jokowi won and democracy survived." *journal of Democracy* 25(4): 111–125.

Mietzner, M. (2014b). Indonesia's decentralization: The rise of local identities and the survival of the nation-state. In *Regional Dynamics in a Decentralized Indonesia*, H. Hill (ed.). Singapore: Institute of Southeast Asian Studies, pp. 45–67.

Mietzner, M. (2015). *Reinventing Asian populism: Jokowi's rise, democracy, and political contestation in Indonesia*. Policy Studies 72. Honolulu: East-West Center.

Mietzner, M. (2018). "Fighting illiberalism with illiberalism: Islamist populism and democratic deconsolidation in Indonesia." *Pacific Affairs* 91(2): 261–282.

Mietzner, M. and B. Muhtadi (2018). "Explaining the 2016 Islamist mobilisation in Indonesia: Religious intolerance, militant groups and the politics of accommodation." *Asian Studies Review*: 1–19.

Miller, J. (2018). *Duterte Harry: Fire and Fury in the Philippines*. Melbourne and London: Scribe.

Moffitt, B. (2015). Contemporary populism and "The People" in the Asia-Pacific: Thaksin Shinawatra and Pauline Hanson. In *The Promise and Perils of Populism: Global Perspectives*, C. de La Torre (ed.). Lexington: University of Kentucky Press, pp. 293–316.

Moffitt, B. (2016). *The Global Rise of Populism: Performance, Political Style, and Representation*. Palo Alto: Stanford University Press.

Mouffe, C. (2005). The "end of politics" and the challenge of right-wing populism. In *Populism and the Mirror of Democracy*, F. Panizza (ed.). New York: Verso, pp. 50–71.

Mouzelis, N. (1985). "On the concept of populism: Populist and clientelist modes of incorporation in semiperipheral polities." *Politics & Society* 14(3): 329–348.

Mudde, C. (1999). "The single-issue party thesis: Extreme right parties and the immigration issue." *West European Politics* 22(3): 182–197.

Mudde, C. (2004). "The populist zeitgeist." *Government and Opposition* 39(4): 542–563.

Mudde, C. and C. Rovira Kaltwasser (2018). "Studying populism in comparative perspective: Reflections on the contemporary and future research agenda." *Comparative Political Studies*. doi: 0010414018789490.

Muhtadi, B. (2018). Buying Votes In Indonesia: Partisans, Personal Networks, and Winning Margins. PhD Dissertation, Australian National University.

Mujani, S., R. W. Liddle and K. Ambardi (2018). *Voting Behavior in Indonesia since Democratization: Critical Democrats*. New York: Cambridge University Press.

Murray, D. (1996). "The 1995 National Elections in Thailand: A Step Backward for Democracy?" *Asian Survey* 36(4): 361–375.

Nelson, M. H. (2001). "Thailand's House Elections of 6 January 2001: Thaksin's Landslide Victory and Subsequent Narrow Escape." In *Thailand's New Politics: KPI Yearbook*, H. H. Nelson (ed.). Nonthaburi and Bangkok: King Praadhipok's Institute and White Lotus Press, pp. 283–441.

Nishizaki, Y. (2011). *Political Authority and Provincial Identity in Thailand: The Making of Banharn-buri*. Ithaca, NY: Cornell Southeast Asia Program.

North, D. C., J. J. Wallis, S. B. Webb and B. R. Weingast (2012). Limited access orders. In *In the Shadow of Violence: Politics, Economics, and the Problem of Development*, D. C. North, J. J. Wallis, S. B. Webb and B. R. Weingast (eds.). New York: Cambridge University Press, pp. 1–23.

Novaes, L. (2017). "Disloyal brokers and weak parties." *American Journal of Political Science* 62(1): 84–98.

Ockey, J. (1994). "Political parties, factions, and corruption in Thailand." *Modern Asian Studies* 28(02): 251–277.

Ockey, J. (2003). "Change and continuity in the Thai political party system." *Asian Survey* 43(4): 663–680.

Ostiguy, P. (2009). The high and the low in politics: A two-dimensional political space for comparative analysis and electoral studies. Kellog Institute Working Paper, 360, University of Notre Dame.

Panebianco, A. (1988). *Political Parties: Organization and Power.* Cambridge: Cambridge University Press.

Pepinsky, T. (2017). "Southeast Asia: Voting against disorder." *Journal of Democracy* 28(2): 120–131.

Phongpaichit, P. and C. Baker (1995). *Thailand: Economy and Politics.* Oxford: Oxford University Press.

Phongpaichit, P. and C. Baker (2008). "Thaksin's populism." *Journal of Contemporary Asia* 38(1): 62–83.

Phongpaichit, P. and C. Baker (2009). *Thaksin.* Second edn. Chiang Mai: Silkworm Books.

Pratt, J. (2007). *Penal Populism: Key Ideas in Criminology.* London; New York: Routledge, Taylor & Francis Group.

Prizzia, R. (1985). *Thailand in Transition: The Role of Oppositional Forces.* Honolulu: University of Hawaii Press.

Przeworski, A. (2004). "Institutions matter? 1." *Government and Opposition* 39(4): 527–540.

Qodari, M. (2010). The professionalisation of politics: the growing role of political consultants and polling organisations. In *Problems of Democratisation in Indonesia: Elections, Institutions, and Society*, E. Aspinall and M. Mietzner (eds.). Singapore: Institute of Southeast Asian Studies, pp. 122–140.

Roberts, K. M. (2014a). *Party Systems in Latin America's Neoliberal Era.* New York: Cambridge University Press.

Roberts, K. M. (2014b). Populism, political mobilizations, and crises of political representation. In *The Promise and Perils of Populism: Global Perspectives*, C. de la Torre (ed.). Lexington, University Press of Kentucky, pp. 140–158.

Robertson, P. S. (1996). "The rise of the rural network politician: Will Thailand's new elite endure?" *Asian Survey* 36(9): 924–941.

Robison, R. (1986). *Indonesia: The Rise of Capital.* North Sydney: Allen & Unwin.

Rooduijn, M., W. van der Brug and S. L. de Lange (2016). "Expressing or fuelling discontent? The relationship between populist voting and political discontent." *Electoral Studies* 43: 32–40.

Rueschemeyer, D., E. Huber and J. D. Stephens (1992). *Capitalist Development and Democracy.* Chicago: University of Chicago Press.

Ruth, S. P. (2015). "Populism and the erosion of horizontal accountability in Latin America." *Political Studies* 66(2): 256–375.

Rydgren, J. (2008). "Immigration sceptics, xenophobes or racists? Radical right-wing voting in six West European countries." *European Journal of Political Research* 47(6): 737–765.

Sartori, G. (1976). *Parties and Party Systems: A Framework for Analysis.* Cambridge, UK: Cambridge University Press.

Schattschneider, E. E. (1942). *Party Government.* New York, Farrar and Rinehart.

Schmidt, S. W., J. C. Scott, C. H. Landé and L. Guasti, Eds. (1977). *Friends, Followers, and Factions: A Reader in Political Clientelism.* Berkeley: University of California Press.

Scott, J. C. (1969). "Corruption, machine politics, and political change." *The American Political Science Review* 63(4): 1142–1158.

Scott, J. C. (1972). "Patron-client politics and political change in Southeast Asia." *The American Political Science Review* 66(1): 91–113.

Shefter, M. (1994). *Political Parties and the State: The American Historical Experience.* Princeton, NJ: Princeton University Press.

Sidel, J. T. (1997). "Philippine politics in town, district, and province: bossism in Cavite and Cebu." *Journal of Asian Studies* 56(4): 947–966.

Simbulan, R. G. (2007). "Contemporary politics in the Philippines: The configuration of post-EDSA I political parties." In *Oligarchic Politics: Elections and the Party List System in the Philippines*, B. M. Tuazon (ed.). Quezon City: CenPeg Books, pp. 22–46.

Slater, D. (2010). *Ordering Power: Contentious Politics and Authoritarian Leviathans in Southeast Asia.* New York: Cambridge University Press.

Stanley, B. (2011). "Populism, nationalism, or national populism? An analysis of Slovak voting behaviour at the 2010 parliamentary election." *Communist and Post-Communist Studies* 44(4): 257–270.

Starner, F. L. (1961). *Magsaysay and the Philippine Peasantry: The Agrarian Impact on Philippine Politics, 1953–1956.* Berkeley: University of California Press.

Steinberg, D. J. (1967). *Philippine Collaboration in World War II.* Ann Arbor: University of Michigan Press.

Stokes, S. C., T. Dunning, M. Nazareno and V. Brusco (2013). *Brokers, Voters, and Clientelism: The Puzzle of Distributive Politics.* New York: Cambridge University Press.

Sukma, R. (2009). "Indonesian politics in 2009: defective elections, resilient democracy." *Bulletin of Indonesian Economic Studies* 45(3): 317–336.

Swamy, A. (2013). "Sources of "Sandwich Coalitions": Distributive Strategies and Democratic Politics in India, Thailand, and the Philippines." *Asia-Pacific Social Science Review* 13(1): 50–56.

Tan, P. J. (2012). Anti-party attitudes in Southeast Asia. In *Party Politics in Southeast Asia: Clientelism and Electoral Competition in Indonesia,*

Thailand and the Philippines, D. Tomsa and A. Ufen (eds.). London: Routledge, pp. 80–100.

Tapsell, R. (2015). "Indonesia's Media Oligarchy and the Jokowi Phenomenon."*Indonesia* 99(1): 29–50.

Thompson, M. R. (2010). "Reformism vs. populism in the Philippines." *Journal of Democracy* 21(4): 154–168.

Thompson, M. R. (2016a). "Bloodied democracy: Duterte and the death of liberal reformism in the Philippines." *Journal of Current Southeast Asian Affairs* 35(3): 39–68.

Thompson, M. R. (2016b). "The moral economy of electoralism and the rise of populism in the Philippines and Thailand." *Journal of Developing Societies* 32(3): 246–269.

Thompson, M. R. (2017). "Duterte's illiberal democracy." *East Asia Forum*, August 7.

Tilly, C. and L. J. Wood (2013). *Social Movements, 1768–2012*. Boulder, CO: Paradigm Publishers.

Tomsa, D. (2010). The Indonesian party system after the 2009 elections: Towards stability? In *Problems of Democratisation in Indonesia*, E. Aspinall and M. Mietzner (eds.). Singapore, Institute of Southeast Asian Studies, pp. 141–159.

Tomsa, D. (2014). "Party system fragmentation in Indonesia: The subnational dimension." *Journal of East Asian Studies* 14(2): 249.

Ungpakorn, J. (2007). *A Coup for the Rich? Thailand's Political Crisis*. Bangkok: Workers Democracy Publishing.

Urbinati, N. (2015). "A revolt against intermediary bodies." *Constellations* 22 (4): 477–486.

van Niekerk, A. E. (1974). *Populism and Political Development in Latin America*. Rotterdam: Rotterdam University Press.

Vickers, A. (2005). *A History of Modern Indonesia*. Cambridge, UK; New York: Cambridge University Press.

Walker, A. (2012). *Thailand's Political Peasants: Power in the Modern Rural Economy*. Madison: University of Wisconsin Press.

Walker, A. (2015). "From legibility to eligibility: Politics, subsidy and productivity in rural Asia." *TRaNS: Trans-Regional and-National Studies of Southeast Asia* 3(1): 45–71.

Weber, M. (1978). *Economy and Society: An Outline of Interpretive Sociology*. Berkeley: University of California Press.

Weiss, M. L. and S. Hassan (2003). Introduction: From moral communitites to NGOs. In *Social Movements in Malaysia: From Moral Communities to*

NGOs, M. L. Weiss and S. Hassan (eds.). London; New York: RoutledgeCurzon, pp. 1–16.

Weyland, K. (2001). "Clarifying a contested concept: Populism in the study of Latin American politics." *Comparative Politics* 34(1): 1–22.

Weyland, K. (2006). The rise and decline of Fujimori's neopopulist leadership. In *The Fujimori Legacy: The Rise of Electoral Authoritarianism in Peru*, J. Carrión (eds.). University Park, Pa., Pennsylvania State University Press, pp. 13–38.

Weyland, K. (2017). Populism: A political-strategic approach. *The Oxford Handbook of Populism*. C. Rovira Kaltwasser, P. Taggart, P. Ochoa Espejo and P. Ostiguy (eds.). New York: Oxford University Press.

Wiles, P. (1969). A syndrome not a doctrine. In *Populism: Its Meaning and National Characteristics*, G. Ionescu and E. Gellner (eds.). New York: Macmillan.

Wilkin, S. (2018). *History Repeating: Why Populists Rise and Governments Fall*. London: Profile Books.

Willner, A. R. (1984). *The Spellbinders: Charismatic Political Leadership*. New Haven, CT: Yale University Press.

Winters, J. A. (2011). *Oligarchy*. Cambridge: Cambridge University Press.

Ziblatt, D. (2017). *Conservative Political Parties and the Birth of Modern Democracy in Europe*. New York: Cambridge University Press.

Acknowledgments

I would like to thank my colleagues and students in the Department of Political and Social Change at the Australian National University. Comments on earlier drafts by Nick Cheesman and Paul Hutchcroft were particularly valuable. Edward Aspinall and two anonymous reviewers for Cambridge University Press offered insightful criticism for which I am grateful. I would also like to thank Oliver Friedmann for research assistance. I thank Ronald Holmes and Pulse Asia Research for making survey data on the Philippines available to me. I also thank Burhanuddin Muhtadi and Bill Liddle and coauthors for sharing Indonesian survey data with me to produce Figure 3. Finally, I thank the editors of the series, Edward Aspinall and Meredith Weiss, for inviting me to make this contribution.

Cambridge Elements ≡

Politics and Society in Southeast Asia

Edward Aspinall

Australian National University

Edward Aspinall is a professor of politics at the Coral Bell School of Asia-Pacific Affairs, Australian National University. A specialist of Southeast Asia, especially Indonesia, much of his research has focused on democratisation, ethnic politics and civil society in Indonesia and, most recently, clientelism across Southeast Asia.

Meredith L. Weiss

University at Albany, SUNY

Meredith L. Weiss is Professor of Political Science at the University at Albany, SUNY. Her research addresses political mobilization and contention, the politics of identity and development, and electoral politics in Southeast Asia. She is active in the American Political Science Association and Association for Asian Studies and has held visiting fellowships or professorships at universities in the US, Malaysia, Singapore, the Philippines, Japan, and Australia.

About the series

The Elements series Politics and Society in Southeast Asia includes both country-specific and thematic studies on one of the world's most dynamic regions. Each title, written by a leading scholar of that country or theme, combines a succinct, comprehensive, up-to-date overview of debates in the scholarly literature with original analysis and a clear argument.

Cambridge Elements ≡

Politics and Society in Southeast Asia

Elements in the Series

Printed in the United States
By Bookmasters